# THE DISCIPLE'S CROSS

## MasterLife

### BOOK 1

Avery T. Willis, Jr.
Kay Moore

LifeWay Press
Nashville, Tennessee

ISBN 0-7673-2579-6
Dewey Decimal Classification: 248.4
Subject Heading: DISCIPLESHIP

This book is text for course CG-0168 in the subject area Personal Life in the Christian Growth Study Plan.

Unless otherwise noted, Scripture quotations are from the Holy Bible,
*New International Version,*
copyright © 1973, 1978, 1984 by International Bible Society.

Scripture quotations marked AMP are from *The Amplified Bible* © The Lockman Foundation 1954, 1958, 1987.
Used by permission.

Scripture quotations marked GNB are from the *Good News Bible,* the Bible in Today's English Version.
Copyright © American Bible Society 1976. Used by permission.

Design: Edward Crawford
Cover illustration: Mick Wiggins

*Printed in the United States of America*

LifeWay Press
127 Ninth Avenue, North
Nashville, Tennessee 37234

# Contents

# The Authors

AVERY T. WILLIS, JR., the author and developer of *MasterLife*, is the senior vice-president of overseas operations at the International Mission Board of the Southern Baptist Convention. The original *MasterLife: Discipleship Training for Leaders*, published in 1980, has been used by more than 250,000 people in the United States and has been translated into more than 50 different languages for use by untold thousands. Willis is also the author of *Indonesian Revival: Why Two Million Came to Christ, The Biblical Basis of Missions, MasterBuilder: Multiplying Leaders, BibleGuide to Discipleship and Doctrine,* and several books in Indonesian.

Willis served for 10 years as a pastor in Oklahoma and Texas and for 14 years as a missionary to Indonesia, during which he served for 6 years as the president of the Indonesian Baptist Theological Seminary. Before assuming his present position, he served as the director of the Adult Department of the Discipleship and Family Development Division, the Sunday School Board of the Southern Baptist Convention, where he introduced the Lay Institute for Equipping (LIFE), a series of in-depth discipleship courses.

KAY MOORE served as the coauthor of this updated edition of *MasterLife*. Formerly a design editor in the Adult Department of the Discipleship and Family Development Division, the Sunday School Board of the Southern Baptist Convention, she led the editorial team that produced the LIFE Support Series, biblically based courses that help people deal with critical issues in their lives. A writer, editor, and conference leader, Moore has authored or coauthored numerous books on family life, relationships, and inspirational topics. She is the author of *Gathering the Missing Pieces in an Adopted Life* and is a frequent contributor to religious magazines and devotional guides.

# Introduction

*MasterLife* is a developmental, small-group discipleship process that will help you develop a lifelong, obedient relationship with Christ. *MasterLife 1: The Disciple's Cross,* is the first of four books in that discipleship process. Through this study you will experience a deeper relationship with Jesus Christ as He leads you to develop six biblical disciplines of a disciple. The other three books in the *MasterLife* process are *MasterLife 2: The Disciple's Personality, MasterLife 3: The Disciple's Victory,* and *MasterLife 4: The Disciple's Mission.* These studies will enable you to acknowledge Christ as your Master and to master life in Him.

## WHAT'S IN IT FOR YOU

The goal of *MasterLife* is your discipleship—for you to become like Christ. To do that, you must follow Jesus, learn to do the things He instructed His followers to do, and help others become His disciples. *MasterLife* was designed to help you make the following definition of *discipleship* a way of life:

> Christian discipleship is developing a personal, lifelong, obedient relationship with Jesus Christ in which He transforms your character into Christlikeness; changes your values into Kingdom values; and involves you in His mission in the home, the church, and the world.

As you progress through the *MasterLife* process and learn to follow Christ as His disciple, you will experience the thrill of growing spiritually. Here are several ways you will grow:

- You will discover that denying yourself, taking up your cross, and following Christ is such an exciting and challenging adventure that it will become the top priority of your life.
- You will understand what it means to abide, or live, in Christ, and you will experience the peace, security, and purpose that abiding in Christ brings.
- You will experience the assurance and confidence that come from living in the Word. You will develop new skills for studying and interpreting the Bible. The Holy Spirit will use those skills to give you fresh insights into the Scriptures and into God's will for your life.
- You will experience new power in prayer as you learn to pray in faith.
- You will experience deeper fellowship with other believers.
- You will discover the joy of sharing Christ with others—both by the way you live and by what you say.
- You will experience the fulfillment of investing yourself in others by ministering to their needs.
- You will observe that Christlike attitudes develop naturally and spontaneously in your life. These include—
  —humility and servanthood;
  —dependence on God;
  —love for people, especially fellow Christians;
  —confidence in yourself and in God;
  —a sense of God's presence through His direct guidance;
  —a desire to serve God and people;
  —concern for unsaved people;
  —deepening faith;
  —overflowing joy;
  —perseverance in faithfulness;
  —appreciation of God's work through the church;
  —companionship with family members;
  —a prayerful spirit.

## SIX KEY DISCIPLINES

As you develop a deeper relationship with Jesus Christ, you will experience His leading you to develop six biblical disciplines of a disciple. These disciplines are—
- spend time with the Master;
- live in the Word;
- pray in faith;
- fellowship with believers;
- witness to the world;
- minister to others.

## THE *MASTERLIFE* PROCESS

*MasterLife 1: The Disciple's Cross* is part of a 24-week discipleship process. Completing all four courses in *MasterLife* will provide you information and experiences you need to be Christ's disciple. Each book builds on the other and is recommended as a prerequisite for the one that follows.

The *MasterLife* process involves six elements. Each element is essential to your study of *MasterLife,* as illustrated in the chair diagram shown.

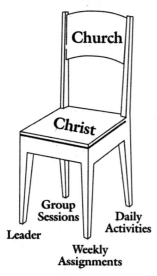

1. The *daily activities* in this book lead you into a closer walk with Christ. Doing these exercises daily is important.
2. The *weekly assignments* in "My Walk with the Master This Week" are real-life experiences that will change your life.
3. The *leader* is a major element. Discipleship is a relationship. It is not something you do by yourself. You need human models, instruction, and accountability to become what Christ intends for you to be. That is why Jesus commanded His disciples to make disciples (see Matt. 28:19-20). We all need someone who has followed Christ long enough to challenge us. To become a better disciple, you need a leader to whom you can relate personally and regularly—someone who can teach you, model behaviors, and hold you accountable.
4. The weekly *group sessions* help you reflect on the concepts and experiences in *MasterLife* and help you apply the ideas to your life. The group sessions allow you to experience in your inmost being the profound changes Christ is making in your life.

Each group session also provides training for the next stage of spiritual growth.

5. *Christ* is the Discipler, and you become His disciple. As you fully depend on Him, He works through each of the previous elements and uses them to support you.
6. The body of Christ—the *church*—is vital for complete discipling to take place. You depend on Christian friends for fellowship, strength, and ministry opportunities. Without the church, you lack the support you need to grow in Christ.

## HOW TO STUDY THIS BOOK

Each day for five days a week you will be expected to study a segment of the material in this workbook and to complete the related activities. You may need from 20 to 30 minutes of study time each day. Even if you find that you can study the material in less time, spreading the study over five days will give you time to apply the truths to your life.

You will notice that discipline logos appear before various assignments:

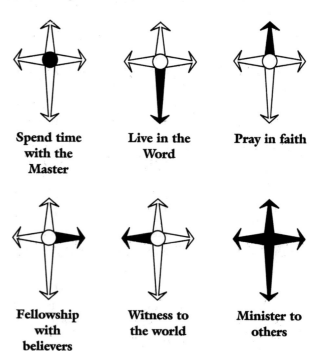

These logos link certain activities to the six disciplines you are learning to incorporate into your life as a disciple. These activities are part of your weekly assignments, which are outlined in "My Walk with the Master This Week" at the beginning of each week's material. The discipline logos differentiate your weekly assignments from the activities related to your study for that particular day.

Set a definite time and select a quiet place to study with little or no interruption. Keep a Bible handy to find Scriptures as directed in the material. Memorizing Scripture is an important part of your work. You will be asked to memorize one Scripture each week. Set aside a portion of your study period for memory work. Unless I have deliberately chosen another version for a specific emphasis, all Scriptures in *MasterLife* are quoted from the *New International Version* of the Bible. However, feel free to memorize Scripture from any version of the Bible you prefer. I suggest that you write each memory verse on a card that you can review often during the week.

After completing each day's assignments, turn to the beginning of the week's material. If you completed an activity that corresponds to one listed under "My Walk with the Master This Week," place a vertical line in the diamond beside the activity. During the following group session a member of the group will verify your work and will add a horizontal line in the diamond, forming a cross in each diamond. This process will confirm that you have completed each weekly assignment before you continue. You may do the assignments at your own pace, but be sure to complete all of them before the next group session.

THE DISCIPLE'S CROSS
On page 136 you will find a diagram of the Disciple's Cross. The Disciple's Cross, which illustrates the six Christian disciplines, will be the focal point for all you learn in this book. Each week you will study an additional portion of the Disciple's Cross and will learn the Scripture that accompanies it. By the end of the study you will be able to explain the cross in your own words and to say all of the verses that go with it. You can learn to live the Disciple's Cross so that it embodies the way you show that you are Christ's follower.

## *Autobiography Worksheet*

Session 1 provides an opportunity for you and other *MasterLife* participants to get to know one another. You will be asked to share your responses to the questions below. Jot down brief thoughts you want to share. Your response to each question should be no longer than one minute.

**1. How have I become the person I am? What person(s) or event(s) have most influenced my values?**

_____

_____

_____

**2. What motivated me to take *MasterLife*? Why do I want to be in this *MasterLife* group?**

_____

_____

_____

_____

**3. What may be my greatest weakness or difficulty in completing the course?**

_____

_____

_____

# Abiding in Christ

This Bible study will help you understand what it means to abide in Christ and will allow you to commit to abide in Christ. Read John 15:1-17. Then complete the following questionnaire. Later, you will share phase 1 with another person, phase 2 with three other persons, and phase 3 with your entire group.

**PHASE 1**
**I find John 15:1-17 (check one)—**
❑ challenging;    ❑ confusing;
❑ comforting;    ❑ scary;
❑ refreshing;    ❑ restrictive;
❑ other: _____

**Imagine that Jesus is speaking directly to you as you read John 15:1-17. He says (check the statements that apply)—**
❑ "I love you" (v. 9);
❑ "You are My friend" (v. 15);
❑ "I have chosen you" (v. 16);
❑ "I have ordained you to bring forth fruit" (v. 16);
❑ "I am speaking to you so that you may have fullness of joy" (v. 11).

**How do you feel when Jesus makes the previous statements about you? Check one:**
❑ Praise the Lord!
❑ Surely You don't mean me, Lord.
❑ I am so unworthy.
❑ Wonderful; let's get on with it.
❑ What's the catch?

**PHASE 2**
**Christ says that if I am to abide in His love, I must keep His commandments. That makes me feel that (check one)—**
❑ He is trying to bribe me into being obedient;
❑ He is sharing His secret for the way He abides in the Father's love;
❑ He is asking too much;
❑ He does not love me;
❑ He really wants me as a friend;
❑ Keeping His commandments is a great way to show my love for Him.

**As I read that Christ has ordained me to bear fruit and that my fruit will last, I feel (check two)—**
❑ thankful;
❑ inadequate;
❑ overjoyed;
❑ strengthened;
❑ defeated;
❑ confident;
❑ enthusiastic;
❑ indifferent.

**PHASE 3**
**To abide in Christ, I need to—**

_____

_____

_____

_____

_____

In response to Jesus' speaking to me through John 15:1-17, for the next week I will concentrate on abiding in Christ by—

_____

_____

_____

_____

_____

# Discipleship Covenant

To participate in *MasterLife*, you are asked to dedicate yourself to God and to your *MasterLife* group by making the following commitments. You may not currently be able to do everything listed, but by signing this covenant, you pledge to adopt these practices as you progress through the study.

**As a disciple of Jesus Christ, I commit myself to—**
- acknowledge Jesus Christ as Lord of my life each day;
- attend all group sessions unless providentially hindered;
- spend from 20 to 30 minutes a day as needed to complete all assignments;
- have a daily quiet time;
- keep a Daily Master Communication Guide about the way God speaks to me and I speak to Him;
- be faithful to my church in attendance and stewardship;
- love and encourage each group member;
- share my faith with others;
- keep in confidence anything that others share in the group sessions;
- submit myself to others willingly in accountability;
- become a discipler of others as God gives opportunities;
- support my church financially by practicing biblical giving;
- pray daily for group members.

Signed _____ Date _____

# WEEK 1

# *Spend Time with the Master*

## This Week's Goal

You will evaluate your discipleship and will focus on Christ as the center of your life.

## My Walk with the Master This Week

You will complete the following activities to develop the six biblical disciplines. When you have completed each activity, draw a vertical line in the diamond beside it.

 SPEND TIME WITH THE MASTER
◇ Tell how to have a daily quiet time and begin to have one regularly.

 LIVE IN THE WORD
◇ Read your Bible every day. Write what God says to you and what you say to God.
◇ Memorize John 15:5.
◇ Review Luke 9:23, which you memorized in the introductory group session.

 PRAY IN FAITH
◇ Pray for each member of your *MasterLife* group by name at least twice this week.
◇ Find a prayer partner with whom you will pray each week.
◇ Use the World-Awareness Map to pray for people throughout the world.

 FELLOWSHIP WITH BELIEVERS
◇ Get better acquainted with a group member.

 WITNESS TO THE WORLD
◇ Demonstrate how others know that you are a Christian.

 MINISTER TO OTHERS
◇ Explain the center of the Disciple's Cross.

## This Week's Scripture-Memory Verse

*" 'I am the vine; you are the branches. If a man remains in me and I in him, he will bear much fruit; apart from me you can do nothing' " (John 15:5).*

# DAY 1

## *The First Priority*

When I went away to college, I had been a Christian for several years. I had done almost everything my church had asked me to do. I had tithed, attended church five times a week, occasionally visited prospects, and read my Bible daily. But when the influences of home and church were removed, I came face to face with who I really was. I realized that I possessed Christ as my Savior but that He did not possess me. I faced the decision, Am I going to be a disciple who gives everything to Christ? I spent many nights walking through the fields near the college, talking to God, and pondering whether I really meant business about being a Christian.

**Am I going to be a disciple who gives everything to Christ?**

Then I started looking at the Scriptures to see what being a disciple involves. The Bible told me that a disciple of Christ is someone who makes Christ the Lord of his or her life. As you learned during your introductory group session, Luke 9:23 says, " 'If anyone would come after me, he must deny himself and take up his cross daily and follow me.' "

I realized that I would be either a real disciple of Christ or a mediocre Christian for the rest of my life. As people often do when they arrive at a crossroads in their walk with Christ, I began to make excuses. I began to tell God that I was not capable of doing all He wanted me to do, that I had failed many times, and that I was not even sure He would want me to be His disciple.

In answer to my excuses, God showed me 2 Chronicles 16:9: " 'The eyes of the Lord range throughout the earth to strengthen those whose hearts are fully committed to him.' " I remembered that evangelist D. L. Moody had heard his friend Henry Varley say, "It remains to be seen what God will do with a man who gives himself up wholly to Him." In response Moody said, "I will be that man."[1] If anyone gave himself up wholly to God, it was D. L. Moody. With only a third-grade education he led hundreds of thousands of people in England and America to God. My response was "Lord, I want to be like that. I want to have a heart committed to You. Then if You do anything with my life, everyone will know it was because You did it and not because of my abilities."

**"Lord, I want to have a heart committed to You."**

My heart has not always been right toward God since that time. However, because of the commitment I made, the Holy Spirit reveals whenever my heart is not right. I immediately confess and ask God to forgive me and to restore my heart.

That is how I decided to be a true disciple of Christ and to commit to a lifelong, obedient relationship with Him. At the outset I said, "I will obey and do whatever God tells me to do, and I will depend on

**This study provides an opportunity for you to reassess your standing in your relationship with Christ.**

Him to accomplish whatever He wants to accomplish through my life." The commitments I made during the following year set the course for my entire life. From that day forward God began to reveal Himself to me and to teach me how to walk with Him. Looking back, I can say that everything that has been accomplished in my life has been because God did it.

This study provides an opportunity for you to reassess your standing in your relationship with Christ. It will help you evaluate yourself as a disciple and take steps to follow Him. Throughout your study of *MasterLife* I will share with you how Christ continued to reveal to me what it means to be His disciple. As I share with you how Christ helped me through my pilgrimage as a student, a pastor, and a missionary and as I share other believers' testimonies, I hope that you will learn the concepts of truly mastering life as Christ lives through you—that you will learn what life in Christ is all about.

WHAT IS A DISCIPLE?

We begin this study by looking at who a disciple is and what a disciple does. The New Testament uses the term *disciple* three ways. First, it is a general term used to describe a committed follower of a teacher or a group.

*"John's disciples and the Pharisees were fasting. Some people came and asked Jesus, 'How is it that John's disciples and the disciples of the Pharisees are fasting, but yours are not?' "* (Mark 2:18).

**Read Mark 2:18 in the margin. The verse mentions three groups or individuals who have disciples. Who are they?**

1. _____

2. _____

3. _____

The persons or groups who had disciples are John, the Pharisees, and Jesus. These disciples were committed followers of these teachers or groups.

Second, the New Testament uses the term *disciple* to refer to the twelve apostles Jesus called. Mark 3:14, in the margin, is very specific about why Jesus called these apostles.

*"He appointed twelve—designating them apostles—that they might be with him and that he might send them out to preach and to have authority to drive out demons"* (Mark 3:14).

**In Mark 3:14 underline the phrases that show two reasons Jesus chose the twelve.**

You probably underlined the words "that they might be with him" and "that he might send them out to preach."

Jesus also used disciple to describe a follower who meets His requirements. For example, He said that His disciples must forsake families, possessions, or anything else that might keep them from following Him.

Read these verses: "Large crowds were traveling with Jesus, and turning to them he said: 'If anyone comes to me and does not hate his father and mother, his wife and children, his brothers and sisters—yes, even his own life—he cannot be my disciple. And anyone who does not carry his cross and follow me cannot be my disciple' " (Luke 14:26-27). Write in your own words what Jesus did when people began to follow Him.

_____

_____

**Jesus said that His disciples must forsake families, possessions, or anything else that might keep them from following Him.**

You likely wrote something like this: He discouraged those who did not commit themselves fully to Him by first stating the requirements for being a disciple. Luke 9:23, the verse I hope you memorized in your introductory group session, also states those requirements.

 **In the margin write Luke 9:23 from one to three times.**

You have seen that the term *disciple* is a general term for a committed follower of a teacher or a group, one of Jesus' twelve apostles, and a follower who meets Jesus' requirements.

## LEARNING THE DISCIPLE'S CROSS

One way you can learn more about what Jesus had in mind for His disciples is to learn the Disciple's Cross, which is the cornerstone of this study. You can see the complete cross on page 136 and can read the presentation of the Disciple's Cross on pages 134–36. When you learn the cross thoroughly, you can use it in a variety of ways. It can help you reflect on where you stand in your discipleship. You can use it to witness. You can use it to evaluate your church. Many churches use the Disciple's Cross to organize their church ministries.

As you proceed through this book, you will study the various elements of the Disciple's Cross. Each week you will learn additional information. By the end of your study you will be able to explain the cross in your own words and to quote all of the Scriptures that go with it.

**One way you can learn more about what Jesus had in mind for His disciples is to learn the Disciple's Cross.**

Begin learning the Disciple's Cross by drawing a circle, representing you, in the margin. Write *Christ* in the center of the circle. This circle will help you focus on ways Christ is to be at the center of your life.

The empty circle you drew represents your life. It pictures denying all of self for Christ. This means that you lose not your identity but your self-centeredness. No one can become a disciple who is not willing to

**DAILY MASTER COMMUNICATION GUIDE**

MATTHEW 6:25-34

**What God said to me:**

_____

_____

_____

_____

_____

_____

_____

**What I said to God:**

_____

_____

_____

_____

_____

_____

_____

deny himself or herself. Christ must be the number one priority in your life.

PUTTING CHRIST FIRST

When Kay Moore, who wrote this book with me, and her husband, Louis, married, they asked their pastor to make their wedding ceremony very personal. The pastor, knowing that their jobs were highly important to both the bride and the groom, wanted them to keep their priorities straight. In their wedding ceremony he wisely cautioned them, "In your marriage your first commitment is to Christ, your second is to each other, your third is to any children who are conceived, and your fourth is to your work."

If someone gave you a similar caution about your priorities, what would be on your list? Do you have a priority above Christ? For some that top priority might be a commitment to a sport. For others that priority might be acquiring material possessions. For still others that priority might be participating in religious activities. Religious activities? you may ask. Doesn't that mean I'm putting Christ first? Not always. Some people can be so involved in "doing church" that they forget the real reason for the activity. Their relationship with Christ may take a back seat to their desire to be recognized for their good works or to meet an inner drive to achieve.

**List the three highest priorities in your life.**

1. _____

2. _____

3. _____

You cannot become a disciple of Christ if you are not willing to make Him number one on your priority list. Stop and pray, asking God to help you remove any obstacles that keep Him from having first place in your life. What do you need to do to give Him first place? List one action you will take to remove an obstacle to placing Him first in your life.

Begin the practice of reading your Bible daily. Today read Matthew 6:25-34, a passage about priorities. After you have read this passage, complete the Daily Master Communication Guide in the margin.

## DAY 2

# *Under Christ's Control*

**Y**ou may believe that you are unusual if you struggle with the issue of priorities. Your family, your job, and other responsibilities demand a great deal of your time. Maybe you think that because previous generations had simpler lives, it was easier for them to focus on Christ and to meet the requirements for discipleship.

If that was true, then why was it necessary for Jesus to remind His disciples, who lived two thousand years ago, that they must give Him supreme loyalty? Luke 14:26-33, in the margin, states that His followers must love Him more than any other person, possession, or purpose.

**Read the Scripture passage in the margin. Circle the parts teaching that Christ must have priority over the following areas of life. Draw a line from the part of the passage to its corresponding area. I have drawn the first line for you.**

Person
Possession
Purpose

Clearly, these areas were concerns in Jesus' day just as they are in ours. In the previous exercise the correct answers are: Possession: "Any of you who does not give up everything he has cannot be my disciple." Purpose: "And anyone who does not carry his cross and follow me cannot be my disciple." The highest purpose is to bear one's cross, which glorifies God. One of the best ways to express cross bearing is by voluntary commitment to Kingdom work that you know is costly.

## A DISCIPLE'S PRIORITIES

Christ's disciples had to learn gradually, just as we do. His followers sometimes put their own selfish needs and concerns above Him. Two of them chose sleep over honoring His request to stay awake and pray with Him in the garden of Gethsemane. They argued about who would be chief in His kingdom. When Jesus was arrested, His followers fled, and one of the closest to Him denied Him. Who was the disciples' first priority on such occasions?

But Jesus never gave up on the disciples, and after His death and resurrection their lives changed dramatically. Acts 4:18-37 shows that His disciples loved Him more than any other person, possession, or purpose in their lives. Jesus never stopped working with them to transform them into His own character. Like them, you can begin to grow now, no matter in what stage of discipleship you find yourself.

**Jesus' followers must love Him more than any other person, possession, or purpose.**

*" 'If anyone comes to me and does not hate his father and mother, his wife and children, his brothers and sisters—yes, even his own life—he cannot be my disciple. And anyone who does not carry his cross and follow me cannot be my disciple. … In the same way, any of you who does not give up everything he has cannot be my disciple' "* (Luke 14:26-33).

## DAILY MASTER COMMUNICATION GUIDE

🕊

### ACTS 4:18-37

**What God said to me:**

_____

_____

_____

_____

_____

_____

_____

**What I said to God:**

_____

_____

_____

_____

_____

_____

_____

_____

✝ Continue the practice of reading your Bible daily. Read Acts 4:18-37 today and ask God to speak to you. Then complete the Daily Master Communication Guide in the margin. Pray about how you will respond to Him. Under "What I said to God" write a summary of your prayer.

The passage you just read indicates that the disciples loved Christ more than any other person, possession, or purpose. Can you say this about your relationship with Christ? Apply this passage to your life. List anyone or anything that presently takes priority over Christ in your life.

Person: _____

Possession: _____

Purpose: _____

As you began to draw the Disciple's Cross in day 1, you learned that Christ should have the main priority in your life, filling up the entire circle of your life as you focus on Him. This priority is necessary for a life-long, obedient relationship with Him.

CHRIST AT THE CENTER

Randy prided himself on the work he did at church. Each Saturday he set up chairs for the Sunday worship service. He served as the chairman of a church committee, taught a weekly Bible study, and helped at all youth events. At least four nights a week he was involved in a project at church. Randy thought that if he did enough at church, people would appreciate and compliment him. When people told Randy that they admired him for his diligent church efforts, he beamed with pride. Soon Randy depended so much on others' praise of him that he forgot the real reason for his service. Randy thought that he was being obedient to Christ by his faithful church service, but his priorities had become misplaced, making his relationship with Christ secondary.

**If Randy drew a circle representing his life, whose name would likely be in the center of the circle?**

_____

**What seems to be the motivation behind Randy's acts of service?**

_____

In the case study about Randy, what looked like service from obedience to Christ was actually service for self. Instead of doing good deeds in Christ's name to serve others, Randy served to gain the approval of others. It could be said that Randy, instead of Christ, was at the center of his circle. Realizing that the focus of our lives is on self instead of on Christ can be a startling revelation, but it is very important to be honest with yourself and with God about this matter.

**Stop and pray, asking God to show you ways other persons, possessions, or purposes motivate you instead of your love for Him.**

**Who or what motivates you?**

_____

_____

_____

**If you listed anything or anyone besides your love for Jesus Christ, confess in prayer that your life is controlled by impure desires. Then list the steps you will take to give Christ control of your life.**

_____

_____

_____

> **Realizing that the focus of our lives is on self instead of on Christ can be a startling revelation.**

To be Christ's disciple, you need to surrender control to Him in every area of life. *MasterLife* will help you with this process.

 Pray by name for each member of your *MasterLife* group. Refer to your Discipleship Covenant on page 9 to recall group members' names.

> **To be Christ's disciple, you need to surrender control to Him in every area of life.**

## DAY 3

# *Connected to the Vine*

**S**o far, so good, *you may think.* I want to have Jesus at the center of my life. I want to adjust my relationship with anyone, anything, or any purpose that takes priority over Him. But I get distracted. I get busy. I forget about Him. I sometimes wait to call on Him until I'm at the end of my rope. How can I allow Him to be the first priority in my life so that I turn to Him first? How can I have a personal, lifelong, obedient relationship with Him?

*" 'I am the vine; you are the branches. If a man remains in me and I in him, he will bear much fruit; apart from me you can do nothing' " (John 15:5).*

*" 'Why do you call me, "Lord, Lord," and do not do what I say?' " (Luke 6:46).*

*" 'This is to my Father's glory, that you bear much fruit, showing yourselves to be my disciples' " (John 15:8).*

*" 'A new command I give you: Love one another. As I have loved you, so you must love one another. By this all men will know that you are my disciples, if you love one another' " (John 13:34-35).*

## REMAINING IN CHRIST

The secret of discipleship is lordship. When you truly acknowledge Christ as Lord in all areas of your life, He lives in you in the fullness of His Spirit. He provides what you need to be like Him and to do His will.

 **Read in the margin John 15:5, your Scripture-memory verse for this week, and complete this sentence:**

**Without Jesus' living in you and your living in Him, you can do _____ to bear fruit.**

You may try to make it on your own. You may try your own remedies and the world's remedies. You may do good deeds to satisfy your ego or to please others. But ultimately, the victory is His. You can do nothing to bear fruit without Him.

**Jesus said that three things will characterize your life when He lives in you and you live in Him. Read the Scriptures in the margin. Match those three things with the appropriate verses.**

|  |  |
|---|---|
| _____ 1. Luke 6:46 | a. obedience |
| _____ 2. John 15:8 | b. love |
| _____ 3. John 13:34-35 | c. fruit |

When He lives in you and you live in Him, obedience, love, and fruit are apparent to persons around you. The correct answers are 1. a, 2. c, 3. b. Remember these three things by putting them in sequence: love produces obedience, and obedience produces fruit.

**In the diagram in the margin write the words *obedience, love,* and *fruit* in the correct sequence.**

## LIFE IN CHRIST

How do you abide in the Vine, as your Scripture-memory verse emphasizes? How do you make Christ the center of your Christian life? Consistently devote part of each day to a quiet time so that you can spend time with the Father and can stay attached to the Vine. Shut out all distractions and totally turn over that portion of your day to Him. If you do not already do so, begin having a daily quiet time to stay in touch with God on a regular, consistent basis.

The two things that will help you grow most as a Christian are a quiet time and Scripture memory. Part of discipleship is setting aside from 15 to 20 minutes every day to spend with Jesus Christ, who is at the center of your life.

 **Here are guidelines for having a consistent quiet time. As you read, write decisions about your personal quiet time. Plan to explain to someone the importance of a quiet time.**

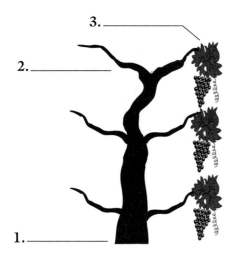

3. _____

2. _____

1. _____

## HOW TO HAVE A QUIET TIME

1. Make a personal quiet time the top priority of your day.
   • Select a time to spend with God that fits your schedule. Usually, morning is preferable, but you may want or need to choose another time.

**My quiet time is/will be _____ every day.**

2. Prepare the night before.
   • If your quiet time is in the morning, set your alarm. If it is difficult for you to wake up, plan to exercise, bathe, dress, and eat before your quiet time.
   • Select a place where you can be alone. Gather materials, such as your Bible, notebook, and a pen or a pencil, and put them in the place selected so that you will not waste time in the morning.

**The place for my quiet time is/will be _____.**

3. Develop a balanced plan of Bible reading and prayer.
   • Pray for guidance during your quiet time.
   • Follow a systematic plan to read your Bible. This course suggests passages of Scripture for you to read each day. Later, I hope that you will develop your own plan. You may want to follow the one provided in *Day by Day in God's Kingdom: A Discipleship Journal.*[2]
   • Make notes of what God says to you through His Word (use Daily Master Communication Guide).

 **For today's Bible passage read Luke 10:38-42. Write your responses in the Daily Master Communication Guide in the margin.**

• Pray in response to the Scriptures you have read.
• As you pray, use various components of prayer. For example, using the acronym ACTS—adoration, confession, thanksgiving, supplication—helps you remember the components.

**Write the components of prayer:**

A _____

C _____

T _____

S _____

---

### DAILY MASTER COMMUNICATION GUIDE

LUKE 10:38-42

**What God said to me:**

_____

_____

_____

_____

_____

_____

_____

**What I said to God:**

_____

_____

_____

_____

_____

_____

_____

**Be persistent until you are consistent.**

> 4. Be persistent until you are consistent.
> - Strive for consistency rather than for length of time spent. Try to have a few minutes of quiet time every day rather than long devotional periods every other day.
> - Expect interruptions. Satan tries to prevent you from spending time with God. He fears even the weakest Christians who are on their knees. Plan around interruptions rather than being frustrated by them.
>
> **Check the days this week you have a quiet time.**
> ❑ Monday ❑ Tuesday ❑ Wednesday ❑ Thursday
> ❑ Friday ❑ Saturday ❑ Sunday

**Focus on the Person you are meeting.**

> 5. Focus on the Person you are meeting rather than on the habit of having the quiet time. If you scheduled a meeting with the person you admire most, you would not allow anything to stand in your way. Meeting God is even more important. He created you with a capacity for fellowship with Him, and He saved you to bring about that fellowship.

LEARNING THE DISCIPLE'S CROSS

Now focus on the Disciple's Cross. Life in Christ is Christ living in you. John 15:5 says: " 'I am the vine; you are the branches. If a man remains in me and I in him, he will bear much fruit; apart from me you can do nothing.' " What can you do without abiding in Christ? Nothing!

Again, draw a circle in the margin. Write *Christ* in the center, and under *Christ* write *John 15:5*, your memory verse for the week, so that you will remember this central premise of discipleship.

Christ said that He is the Vine and that we are the branches. The branches are part of the Vine. We are part of Christ. He wants to live His life through us.

**Is this the kind of life you would like to have?** ❑ Yes  ❑ No
**Describe actions you need to take for Christ to live in you like that.**

_____

_____

You may have answered something like this: I would need to stop watching TV late at night so that I could have a quiet time at bedtime or could get up earlier and have a quiet time in the morning. Or I would need to give up certain bad habits so that I would be a better example of Christ living in me. No matter how you answered, remember Christ's admonition in John 15:5: " 'Apart from me, you can do nothing.' " It does not say that you can do some things on your own. Ultimately, you can do nothing without Him.

**Stop and pray, asking God to help you remove stumbling blocks from your life that keep you from staying connected to Him.**

 **Continue memorizing John 15:5, this week's Scripture-memory verse. Say the verse aloud from one to three times from memory.**

Learning your memory verse is an important part of *MasterLife* because memorizing Scripture is vital to mastering life in Christ. You can recall memorized verses when you need them to strengthen you and to fight temptation.

You also abide in Christ by praying. Find a prayer partner if you have not already found one—someone who is not in your *MasterLife* group. Pray with your partner each week. You can meet to pray, or you can pray on the telephone. In the margin write the initials of someone you are considering to be your prayer partner. Tomorrow you will write the name of the person you selected.

 **Pray by name for each member of your *MasterLife* group. Refer to your Discipleship Covenant to recall members' names.**

> **Memorizing Scripture is vital to mastering life in Christ.**

## DAY 4

# *Learning Obedience*

**O**nce when I was a pastor, a couple in the church disagreed with me and vocally expressed their dislike for me. I unsuccessfully tried to seek reconciliation with them. I finally had to say: "I really want to be your pastor. I value my relationship with God more than anything in the world. To stay in a right relationship with Him, I cannot afford to hold anything against you. I am going to love you regardless of what you think of me."

**List other responses I could have chosen that would not have honored or obeyed Christ.**

> **"I value my relationship with God more than anything in the world."**

I could have made several choices that would not have honored Christ. I could have confronted the couple angrily. I could have said unkind things about them to others. I could have pressured them to leave the church.

I could have been tempted to make any of those choices. In the end, however, I was glad that I stayed connected to the Vine and held to my relationship with Christ as the guiding force in my life. The couple that had been angry with me stayed in the church, and later their daughter was converted and baptized. Because I was obedient to Christ and stayed in a right relationship with Him, the way I responded to the couple bore fruit later.

When you have life in Christ, having completely turned over your life to Him, a lifelong, obedient relationship with Him is a natural result. And when you obey Christ, you want to stay connected to Him and to follow His teachings. As a result of obeying His commands, you bear fruit.

**Stop and review what you just studied about obedience.**

**The key to discipleship is obedience to Christ's** _____.

**Find the following verses and match the benefits of obeying Christ's commands.**

_____ 1. John 15:10          a. You show that you are His disciple.
_____ 2. John 14:21          b. You are blessed.
_____ 3. John 13:34-35     c. The Father loves you and reveals
_____ 4. John 13:17              Himself to you.
                                        d. You remain in His love.

Obeying Christ's commands is the key to discipleship. When you obey these commands, you benefit because you remain in His love (1. d), the Father loves you and reveals Himself to you (2. c), you show that you are His disciple (3. a), and you are blessed (4. b). Christ does not want you to obey Him just to be good; He wants you to be obedient so that He can involve you in His mission.

OBEYING CHRIST'S COMMANDS
*OK*, you think, *that sounds good. I want to obey Christ's commands. I want to have those benefits I just read about. I want to be involved in His mission. But how do I take the first step? How do I start the process of obeying Him?* To obey Christ's commands requires two things: knowing them and doing them. Do you know them? Are you doing what Christ commanded?

**Read the following verses and write in your own words what Christ wants you to emphasize.**

**When you have life in Christ, a lifelong, obedient relationship with Him is a natural result.**

**To obey Christ's commands requires two things: knowing them and doing them.**

1. Matthew 5:19-20: _____

2. Matthew 7:21,24-27: _____

3. Matthew 28:19-20: _____

4. James 1:22: _____

The Bible is very clear about what area Jesus wants you to emphasize. You may have answered something like this: 1. Doing and teaching His commands. 2. Doing His will and practicing His teachings. 3. Observing any or all of His commands. 4. Doing the Word.

**Describe one step you can take to know and do His commands so that you can be obedient.**

_____

_____

You may have answered something like this: I need to set aside time each day to read the Bible consistently so that I will know what the Scriptures tell me to do. I need to develop a quiet time so that I can hear what God is saying to me through His Word. I need to respond immediately when I read Christ's commands or feel His Spirit urging me to obey a command or a Scripture in response to a situation.

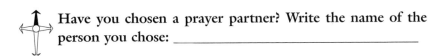 **Continue memorizing John 15:5. Say this verse aloud to someone in your group. Become better acquainted with the group member to whom you recited your memory verse. In the process of getting to know this person, describe in your own words how obedience relates to discipleship.**

**Have you chosen a prayer partner? Write the name of the person you chose:** _____

TAKING ACTION

Have you heard someone say, "Actions speak louder than words"? That admonition also applies to your Christian life. You may know the right thing to do, but what good is knowledge without action? If you are grounded in God's Word but it makes no difference in your life, your knowledge is fruitless. To show that you love Christ, you also need to obey, keep, and do His commandments.

**Stop and pray, asking God to help you begin the practice you listed that will help you become more obedient.**

**To show that you love Christ, you need to obey, keep, and do His commandments.**

## DAILY MASTER COMMUNICATION GUIDE

MATTHEW 26:47-56

**What God said to me:**

_____

_____

_____

_____

_____

_____

_____

**What I said to God:**

_____

_____

_____

_____

_____

_____

_____

_____

Check one or more of the following that you are ready and willing to do.
- ❑ Give Christ first priority in your life
- ❑ Follow Christ by obeying His commands
- ❑ Abide in Christ so that He can produce His life and fruit in you

Suppose you lived in a country that wanted to put you in jail for being a Christian. Would members of a court of law be able to prove that you are a Christian? What evidence would they see in your life, based on the three choices above?

_____

_____

_____

_____

One way you demonstrate that you are a Christian is to follow Christ's command in Matthew 28:19-20, the ultimate demonstration of fruit bearing: " 'Go and make disciples of all nations, baptizing them in the name of the Father and of the Son and of the Holy Spirit, and teaching them to obey everything I have commanded you. And surely I am with you always, to the very end of the age.' " If you follow His commands, you will be aware of the world's needs and will pray daily for those needs.

Study a world map (one is provided on p. 137) or a globe and use it to pray for the world as you listen to news broadcasts, read newspapers and newsmagazines, and read Christian publications like *The Commission* magazine.[3] When you become aware of people who are in crisis and need the Lord, immediately pray for them as an ongoing conversation with Christ.

Continue having your daily quiet time. For your Bible reading use Matthew 26:47-56, a passage about an act of supreme obedience. After you have read this passage, complete the Daily Master Communication Guide in the margin.

# DAY 5

# *Challenges to Obedience*

When we were in the United States on furlough from Indonesia in 1977, I attended many churches that appeared apathetic, showing little vitality in their worship and ministry. This was at a time when our denomination had made a commitment to enlist 50,000 volunteers for short-term mission trips overseas. Having seen little evidence of Christ's lordship in these churches, I could not imagine exporting such apathy to other countries.

God spoke to me in a special way, directing me to return to the United States and make disciples so that our denomination could reach its commitment to share the gospel with everyone in the world. Deeply committed to my work as a missionary and to the work I had begun as the president of the Indonesian Baptist Theological Seminary, I struggled to understand why God would call a missionary from the fifth-largest nation in the world to the United States indefinitely. Week after week in my journal I wrote, "Lord, what are You trying to tell me?" For the next eight months I struggled with God about this matter.

As I preached about Peter's being commanded to eat unclean animals on a large sheet (see Acts 10), I began to see in that sheet the dead churches in which I had been preaching. Although I sensed that God was saying to me, "Rise and eat," I told God that I did not want to get involved with already dead churches and that I wanted to return to Indonesia. I retorted, "Peter had three men at the gate telling him what to do, and I don't have anyone!"

Immediately, three men asked me to do things that applied to my struggle. Our pastor, Tom Elliff, asked me to translate *MasterLife* into English to train his staff. Roy Edgemon, the leader of discipleship training with our denomination's publishing house, asked if I would adapt *MasterLife* for an English-speaking audience. A third, Bill Hogue, the director of our denomination's evangelism program, asked me to help design a plan to train people to witness. I continued to struggle for several months, but finally, God spoke very clearly to me about this matter, as well as about other plans, such as bringing revival and equipping His people to go on mission. Even though leaving Indonesia broke my heart, I knew that I must obey if I was going to teach others to be obedient disciples.

**I knew that I must obey if I was going to teach others to be obedient disciples.**

## COMMITTED TO OBEY

Maybe you are like me. You are not as obedient as you could be or should be. Perhaps you make excuses for not being obedient, as I did. However, read Philippians 2:13 in the margin. Christ created in His disciples a desire and an increasing ability to obey Him. They were ordi-

*"It is God who works in you to will and to act according to his good purpose" (Phil. 2:13).*

nary people, but they had an extraordinary commitment to follow Christ. Again, He did not want them to obey just to be good; He wanted to involve them in His work here on earth.

Examine the following accounts of the process by which Jesus taught His disciples:

1. He commanded, and they obeyed.
2. They learned what Christ was trying to teach them by doing what He commanded them to do.
3. Afterward, Christ discussed with them the meaning of the experience.

**Respond to the following accounts as directed.**

Jesus called His disciples to leave what they were doing and to follow Him. Andrew, Peter, James, and John left their fishing businesses and followed Him (see Matt. 4:18-22). Matthew left his job as a tax collector (see Matt. 9:9). Describe something that would be difficult for you to leave behind or do if God asked you to.

_____

Jesus told Peter to catch a fish, take a coin from its mouth, and pay their taxes (see Matt. 17:27). What would you do if God asked you to do something that seemed unreasonable or that did not make sense to you?

_____

Jesus told His disciples to get a colt for Him and, if the owners asked what they were doing, to say: " ' "The Lord needs it" ' " (Mark 11:3). If Jesus told you to get a pickup truck parked at Main and Broad Streets, what would you do, especially if you had to answer the owner's questions with the statement "The Lord needs it"?

_____

When Jesus told Philip to feed the five thousand, Philip said it was impossible. Andrew offered a boy's lunch even though he did not think it was enough (see John 6:5-11). Which disciple would you be most like?
❑ Philip   ❑ Andrew

Have you ever declined to be obedient because you believed that what God asked you to do was unreasonable or did not make sense? ❑ Yes  ❑ No

The disciples' primary commitment was to be faithful to Jesus. Like the disciples, we are to obey Jesus' commands. Jesus provided resources to help His disciples obey: He prayed for them, sent the Holy Spirit, and provided His written Word. You and I have the same resources available to us. He will provide for us! If you obey His commands, you will experience His love and will bear His fruit. You can have a lifelong, obedient relationship with Him. He will lead your life if you allow Him to do so!

**To review this week's theme, complete this sentence: If your life is characterized by _____, you will experience Christ's _____ and will bear _____.**

If you had difficulty completing the sentence, review the illustration on page 18. As you have studied, you can let Christ lead you and help you so that your life is characterized by obedience, love, and fruit.

## LEARNING THE DISCIPLE'S CROSS

Your primary task is to abide in Christ, the Vine. If you do this, He will be at the center of your life. Below I have drawn for you all of the elements of the Disciple's Cross but have not placed *Christ* at the center of the circle. Fill in the circle and under it write *John 15:5* as a reminder of the Vine and the branches. In the following weeks you will learn more about the components of the Disciple's Cross.

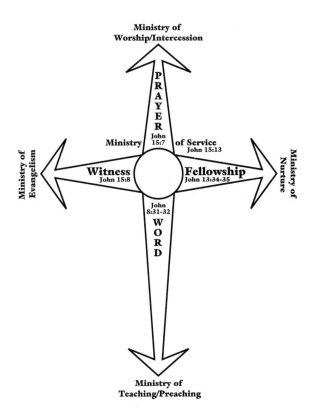

**Like the disciples, we are to obey Jesus' commands.**

## DAILY MASTER COMMUNICATION GUIDE

### JOHN 15

**What God said to me:**

_____

_____

_____

_____

_____

_____

**What I said to God:**

_____

_____

_____

_____

_____

_____

_____

_____

Continue having your daily quiet time. Today read John 15, the chapter from which many of your memory verses in this book will be taken. As you read, look for ways this passage addresses your need to have Christ at the center of your life. Each week I will ask you to read this passage and to look for ways God uses it to speak to that week's discipline. After you have read this passage, complete the Daily Master Communication Guide in the margin.

HAS THIS WEEK MADE A DIFFERENCE?
**Review "My Walk with the Master This Week" at the beginning of this week's material. Mark the activities you have finished by drawing vertical lines in the diamonds beside them. Finish any incomplete activities. Think about what you will say during your group session about your work on these activities.**

Think about your experiences in completing week 1, "Spend Time with the Master."
• Has this week's study made a difference in your life?
• Is Christ more the center of your life now than He was last week?
Pray: "Lord, show me the areas of my life in which You want me to be more disciplined as a Christian" or "Lord, I am weak and need Your strength. Show me how to be disciplined in my walk with You as Master." When you have made the activities of today's lesson regular practices, the Holy Spirit will make a difference in the way you live your life in Christ from day to day.

The inventory beginning on the following page will help you evaluate your Christian life. It was designed for your private use, not for comparing yourself with anyone else. It is not a test, and no one is expected to make a perfect score. Your score reflects how you feel about your life of discipleship as much as it reflects what you do. Although most items are observable acts, one person may interpret his or her actions positively or negatively. You can know a person only by deeds or fruit, but God sees much deeper. Ask God to help you see where you are now and where He wants you to be in your lifelong, obedient relationship with Jesus Christ.

**Read each item and fill in the circle in the column that most nearly represents an accurate evaluation.**

|  | ALWAYS | USUALLY | SOMETIMES | SELDOM | NEVER |
|---|---|---|---|---|---|

**Spending Time with the Master**
- I have a daily quiet time. ○ ○ ○ ○ ○
- I try to make Christ Lord of my life. ○ ○ ○ ○ ○
- I feel close to the Lord throughout the day. ○ ○ ○ ○ ○
- I try to discipline myself. ○ ○ ○ ○ ○
- I am aware that the Lord disciplines me. ○ ○ ○ ○ ○

**Living in the Word**
- I read my Bible daily. ○ ○ ○ ○ ○
- I study my Bible each week. ○ ○ ○ ○ ○
- I memorize a verse of Scripture each week. ○ ○ ○ ○ ○
- I take notes at least once a week as I hear, read, or study the Bible in order to apply it to my life. ○ ○ ○ ○ ○

**Praying in Faith**
- I keep a prayer list and pray for the persons and concerns on the list. ○ ○ ○ ○ ○
- I have experienced a specific answer to prayer during the past month. ○ ○ ○ ○ ○
- Each day my prayers include thanksgiving, praise, confession, petition, and intercession. ○ ○ ○ ○ ○

**Fellowshipping with Believers**
- I seek to live in peace with my fellow Christians. ○ ○ ○ ○ ○
- I seek reconciliation with those who have a problem with me or with whom I have a problem. ○ ○ ○ ○ ○
- Others know I am a Christian by the way I love God's people. ○ ○ ○ ○ ○
- I live in harmony with other members of my family. ○ ○ ○ ○ ○

**Witnessing to the World**
- I regularly pray for lost persons by name. ○ ○ ○ ○ ○

- I share my testimony with others when an appropriate opportunity arises. ○ ○ ○ ○ ○
- I share the plan of salvation with those who are open to hear it. ○ ○ ○ ○ ○
- I witness for Christ each week. ○ ○ ○ ○ ○
- I follow up on and encourage persons I have won to Christ. ○ ○ ○ ○ ○

**Ministering to Others**
- I serve Christ by serving in my church. ○ ○ ○ ○ ○
- I give at least a tithe through my church. ○ ○ ○ ○ ○
- At least once a month I do kind deeds for persons less fortunate than I. ○ ○ ○ ○ ○
- I have goals for my life that I keep clearly in mind. ○ ○ ○ ○ ○

Subtotals ___ ___ ___ ___ ___

x4 x3 x2 x1

Totals ___ ___ ___ ___

Score _____

When you have finished checking each item, add each column except the "Never" column. Each check in the "Always" column is worth four points; the "Usually" column, three points; the "Sometimes" column, two points; the "Seldom" column, one point. Add these four totals together to get your overall score out of a possible one hundred.

**Complete the following statements.**

**I feel that my score (does/does not) adequately reflect my life of discipleship because** _____.

**Other factors that should be taken into account but are not reflected in the inventory and my feelings about them are**

_____.

**My personal, overall evaluation of my discipleship is**

_____.

---

[1] R. A. Torrey, *Why God Used D. L. Moody* (Chicago: Moody Press, 1923), 10.
[2] *Day by Day in God's Kingdom: A Discipleship Journal* provides Scriptures, memory verses, and room to record what you experience in your quiet time. Order item 0-7673-2577-X by writing to the Customer Service Center; 127 Ninth Avenue, North; Nashville, TN 37234-0113; calling 1-800-458-2772; faxing (615) 251-5933; e-mailing customerservice@bssb.com; or visiting a Baptist Book Store or a Lifeway Christian Store.
[3] *The Commission* is a publication of the International Mission Board of the Southern Baptist Convention; P.O. Box 6767; Richmond, VA 23230.

# WEEK 2

# *Live in the Word*

## This Week's Goal

You will grow closer to Christ as you learn to live in the Word by having a daily quiet time and by memorizing Scripture.

## My Walk with the Master This Week

You will complete the following activities to develop the six biblical disciplines. When you have completed each activity, draw a vertical line in the diamond beside it.

### SPEND TIME WITH THE MASTER
◇ During your daily quiet time use the Daily Master Communication Guides in the margins of this week's material.

### LIVE IN THE WORD
◇ Read your Bible every day. Write what God says to you and what you say to God.
◇ Memorize John 8:31-32.
◇ Review Luke 9:23 and John 15:5, which you have already memorized.

### PRAY IN FAITH
◇ Pray for each member of your *MasterLife* group by name.
◇ Pray with your prayer partner once this week. If you do not have a prayer partner yet, find one this week.

### FELLOWSHIP WITH BELIEVERS
◇ Get better acquainted with a member of your group. Visit or call that person. Tell the person that you are praying for him or her. Talk about any blessings or challenges you are having in *MasterLife*.

### WITNESS TO THE WORLD
◇ List the names of at least five lost persons on your Prayer-Covenant List. Begin praying regularly for them. Make any contacts the Spirit leads you to make.

### MINISTER TO OTHERS
◇ Continue learning the Disciple's Cross. Learn the meaning of the bottom part of the cross to add to the information about the circle that you learned last week.

## This Week's Scripture-Memory Verses

*" If you hold to my teaching, you are really my disciples. Then you will know the truth, and the truth will set you free' " (John 8:31-32).*

# DAY 1

## A Close Relationship

**A quiet time is more than merely a habit. It is an appointment with Jesus Christ.**

When I was a young adult, I began trying to have a quiet time. I had read about Christians who got up at 4:00 a.m. to read the Bible for an hour and to pray for an hour before breakfast. I tried to do that, but I could not be consistent. I followed that schedule for a day or two, but then I would be so tired that I could not get up on time. I promised myself that I would try again the next day.

I felt guilty because I could not be consistent. In fact, I almost endangered my health before I realized that the Christians I was reading about were going to bed at 8:00 or 9:00 p.m. I was going to bed at 1:00 or 2:00 a.m.

Soon I read a tract that emphasized spending a short period with God every morning. It stressed the importance of consistency and suggested a simple plan to achieve that goal. I decided that no matter what the circumstances, I would spend seven minutes with God every morning. Of course, I soon realized that was not enough. I continually set the alarm earlier to have enough time with the Lord.

I learned that a quiet time is more than merely a habit. It is an appointment at the beginning of the day with Jesus Christ, who is at the center of my life. I suggest that you begin by setting aside a few minutes every morning with Jesus Christ, for He is also at the center of your life.

Your daily time with Christ is the first of six disciplines that are basic to a disciple's walk. Last week you studied denying yourself and putting Christ at the center of your life as part of becoming a disciple and developing a lifelong, obedient relationship with Him. This week you will begin learning what it means for Christ to be at the center of your life.

### LEARNING THE DISCIPLE'S CROSS

Last week you began drawing the Disciple's Cross to understand what Christ expects of you. You drew the center part to represent the role Christ is to have in your life. As you continue in *MasterLife*, you will draw the cross around the center, one bar at a time, as you incorporate in your life the disciplines that keep you abiding in Christ. You can visualize the cross as representing the six disciplines a disciple needs to practice. Each week your assignments are related to those six disciplines:

**You can visualize the cross as representing the six disciplines a disciple needs to practice.**

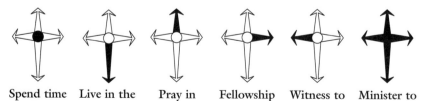

Spend time with the Master | Live in the Word | Pray in faith | Fellowship with believers | Witness to the world | Minister to others

✝ List each discipline according to its position on the Disciple's Cross. Refer to page 32 if you need help.

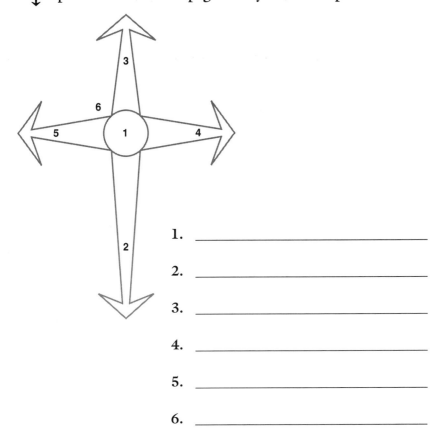

1. _____

2. _____

3. _____

4. _____

5. _____

6. _____

Each week you will add new information about the Disciple's Cross. By the end of your study you will be able to explain the cross and to quote all of the Scriptures that go with it.

Each bar of the cross represents one part of the Christian life. The bottom part represents the Word, and the upper part, which you will add next week, represents prayer. Together these form the vertical crossbar, which represents your relationship with God. In two weeks you will begin drawing the horizontal crossbar, which represents your relationships with others. In your life in Christ you have one Lord, represented by the circle with Christ as the center, and two relationships—with God and other persons.

## REMAINING IN THE WORD

The way to have Christ living in you is to have His Word in you. The first discipline in which you will become proficient is spending time with the Master by having a quiet time. The second and third disciplines, living in the Word and praying in faith, will support your quiet time. Jesus said in John 8:31-32: " 'If you hold to my teaching, you are really my disciples. Then you will know the truth, and the truth will set you free.' " The Word is food for you. You cannot grow unless you regularly partake of the Word.

**The way to have Christ living in you is to have His Word in you.**

✝ **Reread John 8:31-32, this week's Scripture-memory verses. Underline what the verses say about becoming Christ's disciple. Then begin memorizing John 8:31-32 by saying the verses aloud from one to three times.**

You likely underlined the phrase "If you hold to my teaching." Christ's teaching is found in the Word. The absence of regular involvement with His Word keeps you from being the kind of follower Christ wants you to be.

You may wonder: *What difference does it make if I remain in His Word? Won't I still have the same problems as anyone else? Even though I hold to the teachings found in His Word, I will still have sorrows in my life. Will it really matter if I live as a disciple of Christ?* As a Christian, you are not exempt from difficulties. But remaining in His Word cultivates a relationship in which you can successfully weather those storms. When you have a relationship with Christ, He shows you how the Scriptures point to Him as the source of guidance and strength.

A DAILY APPOINTMENT

One way you can know Christ's teaching is through the habit of daily Bible reading, meditation, and prayer. No substitute exists for a quiet time. Persons God has used mightily are those who have discerned God's truth and power in private worship. Joshua 1:8 says of the Word, " 'Meditate on it day and night, so that you may be careful to do everything written in it.' " Memorizing puts God's Word in your head. Meditating puts it in your heart. Meditate on the Word until it is in your heart. With God's Word in your heart you can face any circumstance.

I had a significant experience in a quiet time several years ago. Getting ready for a second prostate surgery, I anticipated that this operation would be similar to the first one I had—although uncomfortable, without any lasting effects. In my quiet time I read Psalm 116:1-9. In verse 3 I read:

> *The cords of death entangled me,*
> *the anguish of the grave came upon me;*
> *I was overcome by trouble and sorrow.*

Becoming apprehensive, I wrote in my prayer journal, "This operation is going to be more dangerous than I thought." I prepared for the worst and then put my confidence in what God said in verses 7-9:

> *Be at rest once more, O my soul,*
> *for the Lord has been good to you.*
> *For you, O Lord, have delivered my soul from death,*
> *my eyes from tears,*
> *my feet from stumbling,*
> *that I may walk before the Lord*
> *in the land of the living.*

**Memorizing puts God's Word in your head. Meditating puts it in your heart.**

After the surgery the pathology report showed one cancer cell. At first I was startled by the word *cancer*, but the Scripture the Lord had given me came to mind and quieted my soul. The doctor said that the cancer cell might be the only one that existed and that he would monitor the situation every three months. I thanked God for His assurance. More than five years have passed since that surgery, and I have had no recurrence of cancer. However, the incident alerted the doctor to discontinue medicine that could have made the cancer cells grow faster.

I thanked God for His gracious warning about the cancer through His Word, which prepared me for the outcome of the surgery. Striving to live a life of obedience did not make me immune to cancer, but my habit of a regular quiet time made me open to a promise from God's Word that helped me get through a trying time with strength and comfort.

**Have you had an experience that led you to closer fellowship with Christ so that you could be more receptive to His direction? ❑ Yes ❑ No If so, describe your experience.**

**A quiet time helps you get to know God through fellowship with Him.**

_____

_____

FELLOWSHIP WITH GOD

The first reason for a quiet time is that it helps you get to know God through fellowship with Him. This week you will study this and three more reasons.

> **REASONS FOR A QUIET TIME**
> 1. **To know God through fellowship with Him**
> 2. To receive direction and guidance for daily decisions
> 3. To bring needs before God
> 4. To bear spiritual fruit

Why do you desire close fellowship with God? To begin with, wanting to communicate with someone you love is natural. Think about the way you feel when you go for a while without seeing or talking to someone you love, such as a parent, a child, a spouse, or a friend. You long to connect with that person once again. You cannot wait for a letter to arrive or to hear the voice on the phone. You hunger for that sweet time of fellowship. When you are a child of God, you have a deep desire for fellowship with your Heavenly Father.

**Read in the margin the verses from 1 John. Then answer in your own words the following questions.**

**Why do you love God (see 1 John 4:19)?**

*"We love because he first loved us" (1 John 4:19).*

*"This is how God showed his love among us: He sent his one and only Son into the world that we might live through him. This is love: not that we loved God, but that he loved us and sent his Son as an atoning sacrifice for our sins" (1 John 4:9-10).*

_____

**A believer and the Father can enjoy the close relationship made possible by Jesus' sacrifice.**

*"[My determined purpose is] that I may know Him—that I may progressively become more deeply and intimately acquainted with Him, perceiving and recognizing and understanding [the wonders of His Person] more strongly and more clearly. And that I may in that same way come to know the power outflowing from His resurrection [which it exerts over believers]; and that I may so share His sufferings as to be continually transformed [in spirit into His likeness even] to His death" (Phil. 3:10, AMP).*

**How do you know that God loves you (see 1 John 4:9-10)?**

_____

_____

You love God as a response to Him: He first loved you. You know that He loves you because He sent His Son to die for you. Failing to return God's love does not influence the way He feels about you. But your love for Him diminishes and grows stale if you do not have the nourishment of daily fellowship with Him. A daily quiet time is important so that a believer and the Father can enjoy the close relationship made possible by Jesus' sacrifice.

**Read Philippians 3:10 in the margin. It is quoted from *The Amplified Bible*, which gives all possible meanings in the Greek language, in which the New Testament was written. Check the benefits Paul received from communion with Christ.**
❑ 1. Knowledge of Christ
❑ 2. Freedom from problems
❑ 3. Resurrection power
❑ 4. Fellowship in suffering
❑ 5. Freedom from death

Christ does not promise that you will be free from death if you commune with Him. He does not promise that your struggles will be fewer. But He promises that you will have knowledge of Him, the power of the resurrection, and fellowship during times of suffering. The correct answers are 1, 3, and 4.

**To summarize what you have learned so far, fill in the blank:**

_____

**The first reason for a daily quiet time is**

_____

When you love someone—and as a Christian, you are to love Christ above all else—you do not want to be separated from that person. You cannot really know someone unless you spend time with him or her. To answer the question in the previous activity, you likely wrote something like "so that I can know Him through fellowship with Him."

Your habit of a daily quiet time strengthens your relationship with the Vine, without whom you can do nothing. Last week's Scripture-memory verse, John 15:5, underscores your helplessness if you are not consistently connected to Christ. He wants to transform your character into Christlikeness as you stay connected to Him.

 Continue memorizing John 8:31-32 and review Luke 9:23, which you memorized earlier. Say them aloud to a family member or a friend.

Continue reading your Bible daily. Today read Matthew 26:36-46, a passage describing a time when Jesus sought solitude for prayer. After you have read this passage, complete the Daily Master Communication Guide in the margin.

# DAY 2

# *Guidance for Daily Decisions*

As you consider living in the Word, the persistent problem of time may surface again. You may think: *Sure, it's good to read my Bible daily. I can try to establish that habit. But living in the Word sounds like something I do around the clock. Does anyone really have enough hours in the day to live in the Word continuously? I have my job, my family, and my other responsibilities. I can't walk around with a Bible in my hand all day.*

Certainly, reading your Bible regularly is a primary way to live in the Word. You need that daily discipline. However, you can receive the Word in many ways besides reading it. These include listening to someone preach it, studying it, memorizing it, meditating on it, recalling it, and applying it. Making Christ Lord and having a personal, lifelong, obedient relationship with Him mean that you want to study and meditate on the Word regularly. Then you live what it says.

**In the previous paragraph underline ways to receive the Word.**

God's Word can permeate your daily life in all kinds of situations. As you memorize Scripture, the verses you learn will surface in your thoughts when you are in various situations. In the same way, you find yourself in countless incidents that require you to apply scriptural truths. Even when you cannot have an open Bible in front of you, you can meditate on verses you have memorized. Hearing someone preach the Word teaches you what God has in mind for you. Developing daily habits of reading and studying the Scriptures helps you live in the Word. In the previous activity you likely underlined all of these ways.

**DAILY MASTER COMMUNICATION GUIDE**

MATTHEW 26:36-46

**What God said to me:**

_____

_____

_____

_____

_____

_____

_____

**What I said to God:**

_____

_____

_____

_____

_____

_____

_____

✝ Take time to work on this week's Scripture-memory verses, John 8:31-32. Say the verses aloud from one to three times. As you go about your activities this week, be aware of times you apply these verses to your life.

LEARNING THE DISCIPLE'S CROSS

✝ To help reinforce what you are learning about living in the Word, draw the portions of the Disciple's Cross you have studied. Draw a circle with *Christ* and *John 15:5* in the center and draw the lower crossbar with *Word* written on it. Now write *John 8:31-32* on the lower crossbar. As you draw, say aloud what you have learned about the Disciple's Cross so far.

One way to get the Word into your mind and heart is through a daily quiet time. Today you will study the second reason for a quiet time.

**A daily quiet time provides direction and guidance for your daily decisions.**

> **REASONS FOR A QUIET TIME**
> 1. To know God through fellowship with Him
> **2. To receive direction and guidance for daily decisions**
> 3. To bring needs before God
> 4. To bear spiritual fruit

ASKING GOD TO SHOW YOU THE WAY

A daily quiet time provides direction and guidance for your daily decisions. You discern God's will as you meditate on His Word and commune with His Spirit. Psalm 143:8 can be your prayer:

*Show me the way I should go,*
*for to you I lift up my soul.*

**In Psalm 143:8 what did the psalmist ask God to do for him?**

_____

_____

**First John 5:14 says, "This is the confidence we have in approaching God: that if we ask anything according to his will, he hears us."**
**What does this verse say about God's response if you pray according to His will?**

_____

**If you pray according to His will, you have the assurance that He hears you.**

Like the psalmist, you can ask God to show you the way you should walk in your life in Christ. If you pray according to His will, you have the assurance that He hears you. I know of no greater reason for taking time to strengthen your relationship with the Vine daily!

FINDING DIRECTION IN THE WORD
God has used His Word to reveal His direction for me over and over again. Once my wife and I were in South Africa leading *MasterLife* training for nine countries. Word arrived that because of a political boycott, no passengers from South Africa would be allowed to disembark in Nairobi, Kenya, where we were to conduct training for another nine countries. We tried to get around this ruling but could find no solution. If we would not be allowed to enter Kenya, we would be forced to proceed to Europe without leading the training.

The day before we were to leave, we decided to go to Harare, Zimbabwe, to get new passports, visas, and tickets in an attempt to travel to Nairobi. On the morning we were to leave, I read in my quiet time Psalm 118. Verses 5-8 say:

*In my anguish I cried to the Lord,*
*and he answered by setting me free.*
*The Lord is with me; I will not be afraid.*
*What can man do to me?*
*The Lord is with me; he is my helper.*
*I will look in triumph on my enemies.*
*It is better to take refuge in the Lord*
*than to trust in man.*

I felt that these verses were God's promise that we would be able to

## DAILY MASTER COMMUNICATION GUIDE

### PSALM 118

**What God said to me:**

_____

_____

_____

_____

_____

_____

_____

**What I said to God:**

_____

_____

_____

_____

_____

_____

_____

_____

enter Nairobi. Verses 14-16 seemed to offer further affirmation:

> _The Lord is my strength and my song;_
> _he has become my salvation._
> _Shouts of joy and victory_
> _resound in the tents of the righteous:_
> _"The Lord's right hand has done mighty things!_
> _The Lord's right hand is lifted high;_
> _the Lord's right hand has done mighty things!"_

We arrived in Harare, Zimbabwe, with only one hour to obtain the new passports, visas, and tickets, but God did it! If you have tried to get any one of those in your own country, you know that what occurred was a miracle. When we reached Nairobi, the officials turned back the three persons in front of us, but they examined our new passports and visas and let us walk through! Shouts of joy and victory resounded from us and from the participants who had prayed that we would be able to enter the country. God had performed a miracle, and I was thankful that I had sought answers from His Word. Without God's assurance, I would not have been bold enough to start on the journey.

**Has God ever helped you make a decision as you sought answers from His Word? ❑ Yes ❑ No If so, describe your experience.**

_____

_____

**To summarize what you have learned today, fill in the blanks below. Check your work by reviewing the list on page 38.**

**The first two reasons for a daily quiet time are:**

_____

_____

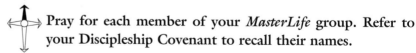 Read Psalm 118 as your Bible passage today and see how God uses it to speak to you. After you have read this passage, complete the Daily Master Communication Guide in the margin.

Pray for each member of your _MasterLife_ group. Refer to your Discipleship Covenant to recall their names.

# DAY 3

# *Petitioning for Needs*

**B**y now you probably realize that remaining in Christ's Word, or holding to His teaching, is not a one-time action. Have you ever read your Bible, closed it, and had a self-satisfied feeling like "Whew! Now that's done"? This is not a task that can be accomplished and then set aside indefinitely. Remaining in His Word, or holding to His teaching, means His Word is so much a part of your life that it is like the air you breathe. Your memory verses for the week are John 8:31-32: " 'If you hold to my teaching, you are really my disciples. Then you will know the truth, and the truth will set you free.' " Today you will spend more time studying the concept of holding to Christ's teaching.

### BRINGING YOUR NEEDS TO GOD

If you hold to Christ's teaching, you will not wait to ask for His help as a last resort. He will be your first source of help. You will seek the Scriptures first when you have needs. This is the third good reason to have a quiet time of reading and meditating on God's Word and fellowshipping with Him. Needs and problems in your life can make you realize your dependence on God. He wants to meet your needs. In a quiet time you can bring your needs before God.

**Today you will study the third reason for a quiet time. In the list below, the first two reasons are blank. See if you can remember them from days 1 and 2.**

> **REASONS FOR A QUIET TIME**
>
> 1. _____
>
> 2. _____
> 3. **To bring needs before God**
> 4. To bear spiritual fruit

**Read the verses in the margin. Match the references in the left column with the prayer promises from the Bible in the right column.**

___ 1. Philippians 4:6-7    a. God renews our strength as we wait on Him.

___ 2. Psalm 34:17    b. In prayer we find grace in our need.

___ 3. Hebrews 4:16    c. God delivers the righteous from trouble.

___ 4. Isaiah 40:31    d. As we make our requests known to God, He gives us peace.

*"Rejoice in the Lord always. I will say it again: Rejoice! Let your gentleness be evident to all. The Lord is near. Do not be anxious about anything, but in everything, by prayer and petition, with thanksgiving, present your requests to God. And the peace of God, which transcends all understanding, will guard your hearts and your minds in Christ Jesus" (Phil. 4:6-7).*

*The righteous cry out, and the Lord hears them;*
*he delivers them from all their troubles (Ps. 34:17).*

*"Let us then approach the throne of grace with confidence, so that we may receive mercy and find grace to help us in our time of need" (Heb. 4:16).*

*Those who hope in the Lord will renew their strength.*
*They will soar on wings like eagles;*
*they will run and not grow weary,*
*they will walk and not be faint (Isa. 40:31).*

These are wonderful promises about what happens when you pray! God provides grace, peace, strength, and deliverance from trouble. The correct answers are 1. d, 2. c, 3. b, and 4. a. Beautiful promises await you if you remain in the Word, as your memory verses, John 8:31-32, remind you.

 **Take a few minutes to review your memory verses, John 8:31-32. Without looking back at page 31, write the verses in the margin to see how well you can recall them.**

By this point in *MasterLife* you may be saying to yourself: *This memory work is tough. I've never been very good at memorizing things.* You may think that you are too busy or too old to begin memorizing Scripture. But Scripture memorization is a major part of remaining in the Word. Being able to recall verses as you need them is important in a Christian's daily walk. Read this story about an amazing woman who overcame challenges to Scripture memorization.

Pearl Collinsgrove of Polo, Missouri, became a Christian at age 79 and began asking to study *MasterLife* after hearing participants in her church talk about experiencing life in Christ. Because Pearl had only a third-grade education and was blind, some church members thought that she would not be able to participate. But one member recorded all of the materials on tape for Pearl, who quickly memorized all of the Scripture-memory verses and many more.

Pearl, a former entertainer, began singing her memorized Scripture verses as she played the guitar. Civic clubs around town invited her to speak and sing. A member of her *MasterLife* group made a cross the same size as Pearl. When she spoke, she showed the cross and sang a song that related to each point and the center. She said, "My feet are planted in God's Word, my hands are lifted up to heaven in worship and prayer, one hand reaches out to my Christian brothers and sisters in fellowship, and the other hand reaches out to the lost world that we need to tell about Jesus."

Word spread about Pearl's testimony, and to rousing applause she sang John 15:5 at the 1985 Southern Baptist Convention in Dallas before 45,000 people. Neither age, blindness, nor a lack of education could deter this fervent woman's learning the *MasterLife* concepts and Scripture verses.

The same God who gives you strength to follow Him at all costs can also give you, like Pearl, the ability to memorize His Word.

 **Get better acquainted with a member of your *MasterLife* group by visiting or calling that person. Talk about any blessings or challenges you are having with Scripture memorization or with any other part of *MasterLife*. Tell the person that you are praying for his or her ability to memorize Scripture and for other needs the person expresses. Together review the verses you have memorized in *MasterLife*.**

**Being able to recall verses as you need them is important in a Christian's daily walk.**

## TRACING ANSWERS TO PRAYER

Another way to stay connected with God is to keep track of the way He meets your needs. Too often we approach His throne with a request but forget to thank Him for the way He answers our prayers. One way to keep track of your requests and answers is by keeping a Prayer-Covenant List. Many Christians have used this system to remind them of what God has done in their lives. Here are some tips on how to use the list.

---

### HOW TO USE THE PRAYER-COVENANT LIST

1. Use the list on page 138. You may want to photocopy the list and make individual lists for various categories of prayer or for different days of the week. Make at least one list of requests for which you pray daily. Pray for other requests weekly or monthly.
2. List each request in specific terms so that you will know when it is answered. For example, do not write, "Bless Aunt Dolly." Instead, ask that Aunt Dolly might be able to use her arm again. Record the date you make the request. If the Holy Spirit at any time impresses on you a Bible verse related to that request, write that verse in the appropriate column. Be alert to verses in your Bible reading that might apply to your request. (Later, you will study more about the different ways God answers prayer.)
3. Leave two or three lines on which to write entries in the answer column. Your prayer may be answered in stages. Write the date when each prayer is answered.

---

✝ Begin keeping your Prayer-Covenant List, using the one on page 138. Make copies of the list provided if you wish. You may want to make a prayer notebook to use as you complete *MasterLife*. At first you may not have enough prayer requests to fill all of the lines. Record only the requests that represent genuine concerns at the time.

Your prayer list with dated answers may become the best evidence you have to convince yourself or someone else of God's concern and power. This was the case for a young construction worker named Dyke Dyer, a member of a *MasterLife* group Shirley and I led at our church in Goodlettsville, Tennessee. Dyke consistently listed his boss on his Prayer-Covenant List as someone who needed salvation. As Dyke reported about his witnessing efforts to the group week after week, we prayed with him, but still no answer came.

Finally, Dyke found a way to take his boss to church and to win him to the Lord. Dyke excitedly told the group, "This is the best thing that has happened to me since I was saved!" It was a joy to see this young man use his Prayer-Covenant List as a means to pray consistently for someone's salvation and to witness this result.

You can not only approach God with your needs during your quiet time but also keep track of how He meets those needs. A quiet time is

---

### DAILY MASTER COMMUNICATION GUIDE

1 SAMUEL 1:9-20

**What God said to me:**

_____

_____

_____

_____

_____

_____

_____

**What I said to God:**

_____

_____

_____

_____

_____

_____

_____

_____

an important habit to develop in your lifelong, obedient relationship with Him.

**Recap today's study by listing the first three reasons for having a quiet time. You will study the fourth reason tomorrow.**

1. _____

2. _____

3. _____

4. To bear spiritual fruit

Pray with your prayer partner once this week. If you do not have a prayer partner yet, find one this week.

Read 1 Samuel 1:9-20, about a person who prayed fervently, during your quiet time today. When you have read the passage, complete the Daily Master Communication Guide on page 43.

## DAY 4

# *Abide and Obey*

**The disciples followed Jesus because they recognized Him as their Master.**

At our family devotional time one day I asked my children why they believed the disciples James and John dropped their nets at Jesus' command and followed Him—no questions asked. My 11-year-old son replied, "They were tired of mending those nets." I do not think that was the real reason the disciples followed Jesus on command. They followed Jesus because they recognized Him as their Master. If you want to sum up discipleship, it is obedience to the lordship of Christ. To remain in the Word, or hold to His teaching, then, means to obey it. You can read the Word, meditate on it, pray about it, hear it preached and taught, and see it demonstrated, but if you do not obey the Word, you have wasted your time.

*" 'If you obey my commands, you will remain in my love, just as I have obeyed my Father's commands and remain in his love' " (John 15:10).*

**Read the verse in the margin and answer the following questions.**

**What happens when you keep Christ's commands?**

_____

_____

**Whose example do you follow when you keep Christ's commands?**

_____

**To abide in Christ means to _____ Him.**

Obeying Christ's commands is the key to discipleship. When you obey them, you remain in a lifelong, obedient relationship with Him. You abide in His love. You obey because of the example Christ set in obeying His Father's commands. When you abide in Him, you obey Him.

How are you doing with your Scripture memorization? I hope that by now you are beginning to experience the benefits of having memorized verses to use instantly when you need them. When I give my testimony, I do not always have a Bible handy. I have found that the Holy Spirit brings to memory exactly the verses that fit each situation. Once when I talked with a woman who visited our church, she made numerous excuses for not coming to Christ. Because I had memorized many verses, the Holy Spirit led me to choose the right verse for each excuse. To each excuse I did not answer a word but asked her to read a verse I had memorized. After she read between 10 and 15 verses, she put her faith in Christ.

**Describe a time when a memorized Scripture proved helpful.**

_____

 Continue memorizing John 8:31-32. Say these verses aloud to someone in your family or to a friend.

Having a quiet time helps you obey Christ's teaching. When you have a daily reminder of what the Bible says, Christ's teaching is fresh on your mind. You do not have to wonder how Christ would have acted in a certain situation; those truths are hidden in your heart. And when you are obedient, you bear spiritual fruit—the fourth reason for a quiet time.

**Write the first three reasons for a quiet time.**

> **REASONS FOR A QUIET TIME**
>
> 1. _____
>
> 2. _____
>
> 3. _____
> 4. To bear spiritual fruit

**You obey because of the example Christ set in obeying His Father's commands.**

**You do not have to wonder how Christ would have acted in a certain situation; those truths are hidden in your heart.**

### BEARING FRUIT

In John 15:4 Jesus said: " 'Remain in me, and I will remain in you. No branch can bear fruit by itself; it must remain in the vine. Neither can you bear fruit unless you remain in me.' "

**What did Jesus say you must do to bear fruit?**

_____

**God does not want you to work _for_ Him. He wants to work _through_ you.**

God does not want you to work _for_ Him. He wants to work _through_ you. His work is accomplished only as you yield your will to Him daily through Bible study, prayer, and meditation. In your lifelong, obedient relationship with Him, He will repeatedly show you how the Scripture points to Him. You can bear fruit only if you remain faithful to the Vine and remain in Him. That is what life in Christ is all about.

Connie Baldwin, a schoolteacher in Virginia, gets up at 5:30 each morning to have her quiet time before she gets ready to teach school. She says this practice helps her bear fruit throughout the day as she works with children and helps her prepare for her job. "Getting up at 5:30 for me is quite a feat because I'm not a morning person," Connie relates. "But I know that God has given me the strength and determination to get up early to spend that time with Him. I know when I get to heaven, I'll never say, 'I wish I had slept more.' I'll say, 'I'm so glad I got up and spent time with my Master!' "

**Jesus was prepared to bear spiritual fruit because His relationship with the Father was always up to date.**

Jesus was prepared to bear spiritual fruit because His relationship with the Father was always up to date. Even when He was tired, He led the Samaritan woman to Christ (see John 4). When He met the funeral procession for the widow's son, He had no time to get prepared. He immediately raised the young man from the dead (see Luke 7:11-12). When He was asleep during the storm and His disciples woke Him crying: "Lord, save us! We're going to drown!" He was ready to act (see Luke 8:22-25).

### KEEPING YOUR RELATIONSHIP FRESH

When opportunities arise, you often have no time to prepare to meet them. But if your relationship has been established during your quiet time and has been kept fresh through prayer and remembering the Word through the day, you will be ready. I am often surprised by what God says to me in my quiet time and by the way it applies to problems and opportunities I face during the day. The next morning, when I review what God revealed to me the day before, I often realize that He had prepared me for the situations that arose.

**Check the opportunities you have had in the past week to bear spiritual fruit.**
❏ **Comforting a friend**
❏ **Witnessing**

❑ Giving advice
❑ Sharing a memory verse or an insight from your quiet time
❑ Praying with someone
❑ Helping a needy person
❑ Encouraging someone
❑ Bearing a wrong action
❑ Controlling your emotions
❑ Loving the unlovely

Review what you have learned this week. Without looking back, list the four reasons for having a quiet time. Draw a star beside the area in which you feel the greatest need for growth.

1. _____

2. _____

3. _____

4. _____

Continue to develop your Prayer-Covenant List by including the names of lost persons. Add the names of lost persons to your list until you have at least five. Begin praying regularly for them. Make any contact the Spirit leads you to make.

Your Prayer-Covenant List can become a living testimony of your living Lord. Once when I was witnessing to an atheist, I showed him my prayer list. I pointed out the date I had asked for seemingly impossible things and the date God had answered those prayers. I said, "If there's not a God, a lot of coincidences happen when I pray." Praise the Lord that He answers our prayers in ways that move even the most resistant person!

In your quiet time today, use Genesis 22:1-19, which focuses on an Old Testament figure who was obedient. After you have read this passage, complete the Daily Master Communication Guide in the margin.

---

**DAILY MASTER COMMUNICATION GUIDE**

GENESIS 22:1-19

**What God said to me:**

_____

_____

_____

_____

_____

_____

_____

**What I said to God:**

_____

_____

_____

_____

_____

_____

_____

# DAY 5

## *A Daily Discipline*

*"Very early in the morning, while it was still dark, Jesus got up, left the house and went off to a solitary place, where he prayed" (Mark 1:35).*

*"One of those days Jesus went out to a mountainside to pray, and spent the night praying to God" (Luke 6:12).*

*"After he had dismissed them, he went up on a mountainside by himself to pray. When evening came, he was there alone" (Matt. 14:23).*

*"After leaving them, he went up on a mountainside to pray" (Mark 6:46).*

**Jesus modeled for us an obedient relationship with the Father.**

In day 4 you studied about following Jesus' example for maintaining your growing relationship with the Father. You might wonder, *Why was it necessary for Him to pray, since He was God's Son?* The reason is that Jesus emptied Himself and became a human being (see Phil. 2:6). He placed Himself in the same relationship with God that we have: that of a learner (see Luke 2:52; Heb. 5:7-9). Jesus enjoyed a unique relationship with God the Father. Although He was God's Son and was filled with God's Spirit, He felt the need to maintain a practice of regular, private worship. He modeled for us an obedient relationship with the Father.

As you can see from the Scriptures in the margin, Jesus established patterns that enabled Him to maintain a special love relationship with God the Father. He prayed in the early morning, during the night without sleep, alone, and when He was away from others.

If Jesus felt a need for regular communion with the Father, we should feel an even greater need. Here is how you can have an effective quiet time.

---

**HOW TO HAVE AN EFFECTIVE QUIET TIME**
1. Schedule a regular time for it.
2. Find a place to be alone with God.
3. Follow a procedure.

---

A REGULAR TIME

Finding a regular time is the first key to an effective quiet time. Having your quiet time in the morning begins the day with a recognition of your dependence on God and His all-sufficiency. It gives you an opportunity to yield your will to Him and consciously dedicate the day to His glory.

**What time do you usually get up in the morning?** _____
**What adjustments would you need to make to get up 15 minutes earlier tomorrow morning?**

_____

_____

I believe it is important to meet with God in the morning so that you consciously seek His guidance and hear His word for the day. However, some Christians find that a quiet time at bedtime eases the tensions of the day, provides a peaceful prelude to rest, and prepares them for the next day. The important factor is that the time be daily and regular so that it becomes a habit.

**Do you have a time of day when you habitually pray? ❑ Yes ❑ No If not, make a commitment to schedule a quiet time at _____ ❑ a.m. ❑ p.m. each day.**

## A QUIET PLACE

A second requirement for an effective quiet time is a place where you can be alone with God. Matthew 6:6, in the margin, describes how Jesus encouraged His followers to pray. Most people find that they can concentrate best when they have an established place away from noise, distractions, and other people—a place like a bedroom, study, den, or garage—where they can focus on the One to whom they are praying.

*" 'When you pray, go into your room, close the door and pray to your Father, who is unseen. Then your Father, who sees what is done in secret, will reward you' " (Matt. 6:6).*

**Name the best place for you to have a quiet time: _____**

## A PROCEDURE TO FOLLOW

A third requirement for an effective quiet time is to follow a procedure. Unless you consciously follow a pattern that keeps your mind focused on spiritual matters, you will probably find that your mind tends to wander.

**The following elements may be included in your quiet time. Check the ones you are currently using.**
❑ **Fellowshipping with God in prayer**
❑ **Bible reading or study**
❑ **Praying through the day's schedule**
❑ **Memorizing and/or reviewing memory verses**
❑ **Praying through your prayer list(s)**
❑ **Studying the day's *MasterLife* assignment**

❑ **Other: _____**

**Unless you consciously follow a pattern that keeps your mind focused on spiritual matters, you will probably find that your mind tends to wander.**

The following is my personal procedure. You may want to adapt it to determine your procedure.
1. I kneel in prayer and renew my relationship with God after the night's rest. During this time I often use the ACTS model on page 19.
2. After fellowshipping with God, I sit or kneel and read Scripture. I usually read a chapter a day as I read consecutively through a book of the Bible. During *MasterLife* I suggest that you read Scriptures related to the day's lesson. Later, you will determine which book of the Bible to read and how much to read each day.
3. While I read or after I have finished reading, I summarize in my journal what God said to me and what I said to God.

**Use your Prayer-Covenant List to pray for the requests listed.**

4. I use my Prayer-Covenant List to pray for the requests listed. I add other subjects God leads me to pray about.

You may use my procedure or may develop another. Perhaps you could try several different ways to organize your quiet time in the next several days to see which one you are most comfortable with and which helps you best relate to God.

**Write the procedure you want to use in tomorrow's quiet time.**

_____

_____

_____

_____

_____

**To recap what you have studied today, explain the significance of the three requirements for a quiet time. Check your answers by reviewing what you have read.**

**A regular time:** _____

_____

_____

_____

**A quiet place:** _____

_____

_____

_____

**A procedure to follow:** _____

_____

_____

_____

LEARNING THE DISCIPLE'S CROSS

In this week's Scripture-memory verses, John 8:31-32, Jesus said that His disciples are characterized by holding to His teaching.

To demonstrate that you understand the importance of remaining in His Word, or holding to His teaching, as a characteristic of a disciple, draw the portions of the Disciple's Cross you have studied so far. Draw the circle, the lower crossbar, and the words and verses that go in them. Explain mentally or aloud what you have learned about the Disciple's Cross this week.

First Peter 2:5 refers to believers as priests who may "offer up spiritual sacrifices, acceptable to God by Jesus Christ." As priests, we have the privilege and responsibility to worship the Lord daily.

**As priests, we have the privilege and responsibility to worship the Lord daily.**

## DAILY MASTER COMMUNICATION GUIDE

### JOHN 15

**What God said to me:**

_____

_____

_____

_____

_____

_____

_____

**What I said to God:**

_____

_____

_____

_____

_____

_____

_____

Evaluate the degree to which you do the following by filling in the circles in the appropriate columns.

|  | ALWAYS | USUALLY | SOMETIMES | SELDOM | NEVER |
|---|---|---|---|---|---|
| Have a regular time | ○ | ○ | ○ | ○ |  |
| Have an established place to meet God | ○ | ○ | ○ | ○ |  |
| Have a procedure to follow | ○ | ○ | ○ | ○ |  |

Enabling sinful people to commune with God cost Him His only Son. Yet God was willing to pay that price to have relationships with us. Part of your life in Christ is daily communication with the Father. What is it costing you to have fellowship with Him?

**Will you give God at least 15 minutes daily, starting tomorrow?** ❏ Yes ❏ No If this is your desire, tell Him so now in a prayer.

Again read John 15 in your quiet time today. This time look for ways God uses this passage to speak to you about remaining in His Word, or holding to His teaching. After you have read this passage, complete the Daily Master Communication Guide in the margin.

HAS THIS WEEK MADE A DIFFERENCE?
**Review "My Walk with the Master This Week" at the beginning of this week's material. Mark the activities you have finished by drawing vertical lines in the diamonds beside them. Finish any incomplete activities. Think about what you will say during your group session about your work on these activities.**

As you complete your study of "Live in the Word," think about the experiences you have had this week.
- Are you truly becoming a disciple, as John 8:31-32 describes?
- Have you observed growth in your life this week as a result of what you learned?
- Are you abiding in Christ more this week than you were last week?
- Have you progressed in developing a personal, lifelong, obedient relationship with Him?

_MasterLife_ encourages you not to stand still in your life in Christ but to move forward. You would not be participating in this study if you wanted only to stand still. I pray that God is working through your experiences to help you grow as a disciple.

# WEEK 3

## *Pray in Faith*

## This Week's Goal
You will grow in your relationship with Christ by praying in faith.

## My Walk with the Master This Week
You will complete the following activities to develop the six biblical disciplines.
When you have completed each activity, draw a vertical line in the diamond beside it.

 SPEND TIME WITH THE MASTER
◇ Have a quiet time every day, using the Daily Master Communication Guides
in the margins of this week's material.

 LIVE IN THE WORD
◇ Read your Bible every day. Write what God says to you and what you say
to God.
◇ Memorize John 15:7.
◇ Review Luke 9:23, John 15:5, and John 8:31-32.

 PRAY IN FAITH
◇ Pray for each member of your *MasterLife* group by name.
◇ Pray with your prayer partner in person or by telephone.
◇ Pray for the needs on your Prayer-Covenant List.

 FELLOWSHIP WITH BELIEVERS
◇ Share with someone your testimony of having a quiet time.

 WITNESS TO THE WORLD
◇ Show God's love to a person who is not a Christian.

 MINISTER TO OTHERS
◇ Continue learning the Disciple's Cross. Learn the meaning of the top part of
the cross and memorize the Scripture that goes with it. Be ready to explain
the top and bottom parts of the cross to someone in your group at the next
session.

## This Week's Scripture-Memory Verse
*" 'If you remain in me and my words remain in you, ask whatever you wish, and it
will be given you' " (John 15:7).*

# DAY 1

~

# *Praying for What God Wants*

**God began to teach me to pray in faith.**

When I was in college, God began to teach me to pray in faith. I read a sermon by evangelist Gypsy Smith based on John 15:7, your memory verse for this week: " 'If you remain in me and my words remain in you, ask whatever you wish, and it will be given you.' " It impressed me so much that I said to God: "Lord, I'm trying my best to abide in you. I ought to be able to ask anything and have my prayer answered because You promised it." I then felt impressed to pray that someone would trust Christ as Savior as I witnessed on the street that night. I wrote in my diary, "I believe that someone will be saved tonight (John 15:7)."

I went out on the street and began inviting people to attend services at the rescue mission. When two men accompanied me, I thought: *That's great. Maybe two are going to be saved tonight.* But when the sermon was over, I turned to them and asked, "Are you Christians?" They both said, "Yes." I could not understand that, because I had prayed that God would save someone. After the service I looked for someone else to whom I could witness but did not find anyone. On the way home my mind was bombarded by questions. I said: "Lord, as far as I know, I am abiding in You as John 15:7 says. Why haven't You answered as You promised? Isn't Your Word true?"

When I got back to campus, I remembered that I had forgotten to bring home a friend's coat for which I was responsible. When I went back for the coat, I decided once more to try to find someone to whom I could witness. I met an 18-year-old man standing on the street corner. After I explained how to be saved, he gave his life to Christ. I praised God for the man's salvation, and I rejoiced that His Word was true and that He did what He promised. Even before the man was baptized, he led someone else to Christ.

**I rejoiced that His Word was true and that He did what He promised.**

Eager to press on with my new understanding of prayer and faith, I remembered that I would preach the next Sunday night at the church in Tulsa where my father was the pastor. I seldom pray for exact numbers of persons to be saved, but I felt the Holy Spirit impressing me to ask that five persons be converted as I preached. At that time five persons had never made decisions when I preached unless they were decisions to leave! I said, "God, I believe your Word that you will save five persons." When I arrived in Tulsa, I asked my dad to give me prospect cards so that I could make visits, knowing that only if unsaved persons were at church could they be saved in the service. When the night arrived and I gave the invitation, five persons walked down the aisles to accept Christ, and another rededicated his life. I began to realize that God really wanted to do something if I prayed in accordance with His will.

The next week I went even a step farther. I asked God, "What about 10 persons this weekend?" But this time nothing happened, because God wanted me to learn an even more important lesson about prayer. This time people were not saved because I had begun trying to tell God what I wanted rather than praying on the basis of what He revealed. I learned that prayer is intended to involve me in God's purpose rather than my involving Him in my plans.

**Think of a time when you prayed on the basis of what you wanted rather than seeking God's will first. Describe this experience below.**

_____

_____

## ASKING ACCORDING TO HIS WILL

God delights in answering prayer that is asked according to His will, but He refuses to answer prayer that is not consistent with what He wants. We need to hear God's voice so that we will know what to pray.

Most people are not asked to make the sacrifices Alex and Shelby Credle made, although all need to deny self to follow Him. Alex was a business executive who earned a large income and had job security. His wife, Shelby, was a college instructor who found meaning in her work teaching communications. They lived in a prosperous subdivision in North Carolina, and their grandchildren lived nearby. Yet Alex and Shelby quit their jobs, sold their home, gave away most of their possessions, and departed for Asia, where they began working for a humanitarian organization to share their faith. The Credles said they took this drastic step joyfully because they wanted to follow God's will for their lives.

The Credles had relocated many times during the course of Alex's employment, but one thing made this move different. "It's the first time we've ever prayed about a move and sought God's Word to guide us," said Shelby. "We've always gone it alone before." The Credles stayed close to the Vine and prayed in faith during their decision. This gave them the courage and confidence to make a major lifestyle change.

You may ask, _If I pray on the basis of what God wants rather than what I want, will I have to do what the Credles did?_ Their case is rare. The important question to ask is, _Am I willing to pray as the Credles did?_

**Do you read God's Word for direction and pray in faith when you need to make a major decision?**
- ❏ Yes, I always do this.
- ❏ I try to do this most of the time.
- ❏ I know I should, but I don't as often as I'd like.
- ❏ I usually consult God after I've made the decision.

**We need to hear God's voice so that we will know what to pray.**

**DAILY MASTER COMMUNICATION GUIDE**

MATTHEW 14:22-36

**What God said to me:**

_____

_____

_____

_____

_____

_____

**What I said to God:**

_____

_____

_____

_____

_____

_____

_____

Turn back to page 53 and read aloud John 15:7, your memory verse for the week. Write what you think this verse says about consulting God first when making a decision. Meditate on the verse. Ask God to show you what He wants and to give you faith to believe that He will do it.

LEARNING THE DISCIPLE'S CROSS

In _MasterLife_ you are learning the disciplines around the Disciple's Cross. The first discipline you studied was spending time with the Master and keeping Him at the center of your life. Last week you studied the second discipline: living in the Word. A third discipline a disciple must practice is praying in faith. This week you will learn the role of prayer in keeping Christ at the center of your life.

To preview what you will learn this week about praying in faith, draw the portions of the Disciple's Cross you have studied. Draw a circle with _Christ_ in the center and draw the lower crossbar with _Word_ written on it. Add the verses that apply. Then draw the upper crossbar with _prayer_ written on it. Refer to the completed Disciple's Cross on page 136 if you need help with your drawing.

The center of the cross represents one Lord, since He is the first priority in your life. The bars of the cross represent two relationships. _Word_ on the bottom and _prayer_ on the top, forming the vertical crossbar, represent your relationship with Christ. The horizontal crossbar represents your relationships with others.

> **Continue reading your Bible daily during your quiet time. Today read Matthew 14:22-36, a passage describing a time when Jesus went away to pray. After you have read this passage, complete the Daily Master Communication Guide on page 56.**

# DAY 2

## Enter His Gates with Thanksgiving

As you studied day 1, you may have said to yourself: I'd really like to learn to pray like that. But how do I begin? How do I know the right way to talk to the Father? Maybe in the past you have prayed by reciting words you have memorized. Or maybe your prayers have merely been lists of requests rather than meaningful conversations with God. If you want to go deeper in your prayer life, you can learn to pray in faith as you develop your personal, lifelong, obedient relationship with Him.

### ENTERING GOD'S PRESENCE

The Old Testament teaches that prayer is an act of actually coming into God's presence. If you think about prayer as a way to enter God's presence, you can understand why amazing things can happen when you pray.

Biblical comparisons of heaven and the temple can help you focus on entering God's presence. In Isaiah 6:1-3, in the margin, the prophet Isaiah depicted heaven as the temple. As Isaiah came into God's presence, he saw the train of God's robe filling the temple. Witnessing God's majesty, Isaiah experienced the holiness of His presence.

**In Isaiah 6:1-3 underline words or phrases that describe how Isaiah viewed God during this experience.**

Isaiah obviously became aware of God's awesome holiness. You may have underlined the words high, exalted, holy, and the whole earth is full of his glory.

When you pray, you too can imagine entering the temple as you approach God and experience His awesome holiness. The drawing in the margin gives you a general idea of what the temple in Jerusalem looked like. The temple provided various levels of access, beginning with the gates and culminating with the holy of holies. Each level suc-

*"In the year that King Uzziah died, I saw the Lord seated on a throne, high and exalted, and the train of his robe filled the temple. Above him were seraphs, each with six wings: With two wings they covered their faces, with two they covered their feet, and with two they were flying. And they were calling to one another:*
*'Holy, holy, holy is the Lord Almighty;*
*  the whole earth is full of his glory' " (Isa. 6:1-3).*

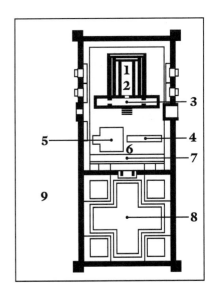

1. Holy of holies
2. Holy place
3. Porch
4. Slaughterhouse
5. Altar
6. Court of priests
7. Court of Israel
8. Court of women
9. Court of Gentiles

*"Since we have a great high priest who has gone through the heavens, Jesus the Son of God, let us hold firmly to the faith we profess. For we do not have a high priest who is unable to sympathize with our weaknesses, but we have one who has been tempted in every way, just as we are—yet was without sin. Let us then approach the throne of grace with confidence, so that we may receive mercy and find grace to help us in our time of need" (Heb. 4:14-16).*

*Enter his gates with thanksgiving*
*and his courts with praise;*
*give thanks to him and praise his name (Ps. 100:4).*

*These things I remember*
*as I pour out my soul:*
*how I used to go with the multitude,*
*leading the procession to the house of God,*
*with shouts of joy and thanksgiving*
*among the festive throng (Ps. 42:4).*

*I will praise God's name in song*
*and glorify him with thanksgiving.*
*This will please the Lord more than an ox,*
*more than a bull with its horns and hoofs (Ps. 69:30-31).*

cessively limited access to groups of people. In Bible times a layperson could enter only certain areas of the temple.

Only the high priest was permitted to enter the area that contained the holy of holies—the most sacred place and the innermost part of the temple. But Christ provided a way for all people to enter the holy of holies and to have an intimate relationship with God through prayer. His death on the cross broke through the limitations of earthly life, making it possible for you to enjoy direct access to God. Because Christ came to earth as a human being, His atoning death brought an end to the priests' role. He now represents you as your Great High Priest before God.

**Read Hebrews 4:14-16 in the margin.**

APPROACHING GOD

Although the holy of holies had limited access, the large, open court-yard at the edge of the temple was open to everyone. As people entered through those beautiful temple gates, they gave thanks. The verses from Psalms in the margin help you picture how the people approached the temple with thanksgiving. When you approach God, it is not proper to rush into His presence and bombard Him with your needs. First, thank Him for all He has done for you. Thanksgiving is the way to approach God.

T. W. Hunt, the author of *Disciple's Prayer Life,* described how he became aware of his need for an expanded attitude of thanksgiving. One morning as he brushed his teeth, T. W. asked himself, *What if tomorrow I had only the things for which I thanked God today?* He began to name things like his teeth, his eyes, the sense of touch, air, home, people—items he realized he sometimes took for granted. He changed his approach to prayer so that he began with thanksgiving to God.

**What are things you take for granted for which you want to begin thanking God? Start now by writing a prayer thanking God for some of these items.**

**Thank You, God, for—**

_____

_____

_____

In thanksgiving you express gratitude toward God, generally in response to His concrete acts. Psalm 69:30-31, in the margin, shows the value God places on your prayers of thankfulness. He values prayers of thanksgiving more than acts of sacrifice.

What kinds of things do you thank God for? The psalms, in which an attitude of thankfulness is especially prominent, give examples of areas in which you can give thanks.

- **Deliverance from trouble:**

  *The angel of the Lord encamps around those who fear him,*
  *        and he delivers them.*
  *Taste and see that the Lord is good;*
  *        blessed is the man who takes refuge in him (Ps. 34:7).*

- **God's faithfulness:**

  *The Lord is good and his love endures forever;*
  *        his faithfulness continues through all generations*
  *(Ps. 100:5).*

- **Forgiveness of sin:**

  *Sing to the Lord, you saints of his;*
  *        praise his holy name.*
  *For his anger lasts only a moment,*
  *        but his favor lasts a lifetime (Ps. 30:4-5).*

- **Creation:**

  *You make me glad by your deeds, O Lord;*
  *        I sing for joy at the works of your hands (Ps. 92:4).*

**Does that list prompt you to remember things for which you need to be thankful? Go back and draw a star beside one area in which you need to express gratitude. Then stop and pray, thanking God for what He brought to mind.**

You can get so busy presenting your requests to God that you neglect a time of thankfulness. What about earlier requests He answered? True, not everything you have asked for is granted. You may be waiting for an answer. Sometimes the answer you wanted was not part of His plan, and He gave you an answer that was better for you than the one you desired. But He certainly answers many of your requests just as you asked. How many of them have you thanked Him for? Your Prayer-Covenant List is an obvious record of answered prayer. In the brief time you have kept a Prayer-Covenant List, what answers to prayer have you recorded?

**Stop and review your Prayer-Covenant List or a list you kept previously. List two prayer requests for which you have already seen answers. Then enter God's presence and thank Him for them.**

## DAILY MASTER COMMUNICATION GUIDE

### JOHN 15

**What God said to me:**

_____

_____

_____

_____

_____

_____

_____

**What I said to God:**

_____

_____

_____

_____

_____

_____

_____

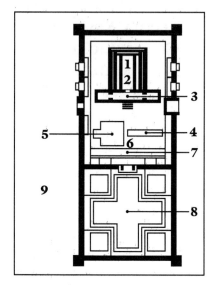

1. Holy of holies
2. Holy place
3. Porch
4. Slaughterhouse
5. Altar
6. Court of priests
7. Court of Israel
8. Court of women
9. Court of Gentiles

Prayer is the discipline you are studying this week. A part of life in Christ is praying in faith. Jesus said in John 15:7, " 'If you remain in me and my words remain in you, ask whatever you wish, and it will be given you.' "

 Stop and review John 15:7, your memory verse you just read. Say it to your prayer partner in person or by phone during your prayer time this week. Also say the verses you memorized previously.

Again read John 15 as your Bible passage today. As you read the passage this time, look for ways God uses it to speak to you about praying in faith. After you have read this passage, complete the Daily Master Communication Guide on page 59.

# DAY 3

## *Enter His Courts with Praise*

The next step in learning to pray in faith involves focusing on who the Father is and what He means in your life. Jesus did not just teach His disciples how to pray. He taught them how to know the Father through prayer. Focusing on Him will continue to set the pace for your quiet time. It will help you overcome distractions or demands to acknowledge the One whose throne you are approaching. It will help you communicate with Him. Set other thoughts aside as you continue to make a deliberate effort to concentrate on the Father.

Again, think about the way people approached the temple in Jerusalem in Bible times as you consider how to approach God's throne in prayer. As the people entered the courts of the temple, they came with praise, as Psalm 100:4, in the margin, indicates. Praise is based on adoration of God. Adoration is what you do in worship.

*Enter his gates with thanksgiving and his courts with praise; give thanks to him and praise his name (Ps. 100:4).*

### PROCLAIMING HIS WORTH

The word *praise* originates from a Latin word meaning *value* or *price*. Thus, to give praise to God is to proclaim His merit or worth. How you do this—whether you are kneeling, standing, sitting, or reclining—does not matter. John 11:41 implies that Jesus prayed with His eyes open. Regardless of how you praise Him and under what circumstances, praise is an important element of prayer. It is to be constant, as Psalm 34:1, in the margin, indicates. Praise raises your prayer life above yourself.

Praise focuses on the person of God. Some of God's names that appear in the Bible reveal His character—ways He works in your life. You can praise God as you recognize the aspects of His character that are revealed in His names. To discover various aspects of God's character, study Psalm 91, which mentions several of His names.

 **During your quiet time read Psalm 91. After you have read this passage, complete the Daily Master Communication Guide on page 62.**

Here are the names of God that are used in Psalm 91:

*El Elyon:*

> *He who dwells in the shelter of the Most High*
> *will rest in the shadow of the Almighty (Ps. 91:1).*

The term *Most High* reveals the name *El Elyon,* the strongest of all gods and the possessor of heaven and earth—the strongest of the strong. Do you believe that you win the daily battles of life in your own strength? The true victory originates with *El Elyon.* He is capable of arranging even the most tedious details of your life.

**Think about a time when you experienced the characteristic of God revealed by the name *El Elyon.* Has He worked out a circumstance in your life beyond anything you could have imagined? ❑ Yes ❑ No If so, describe this experience below. Stop and praise God as *El Elyon,* the Most High God.**

---

*El Shaddai:*

> *He who dwells in the shelter of the Most High*
> *will rest in the shadow of the Almighty (Ps. 91:1).*

The term *Almighty* reveals the name *El Shaddai,* the all-sufficient God. The name is first used in Genesis 17:1, when God appeared to Abraham and made great promises to Him. God promised to make of him a great nation and to give him a son at his advanced age. God keeps His promises. Read Romans 4:20-21 in the margin.

**Think about a time when you experienced the characteristic of God revealed by the name *El Shaddai.* Can you think of an occasion**

*I will extol the Lord at all times;*
*his praise will always be on my lips (Ps. 34:1)*

*"He did not waver through unbelief regarding the promise of God, but was strengthened in his faith and gave glory to God, being fully persuaded that God had power to do what he had promised" (Rom. 4:20-21).*

## DAILY MASTER COMMUNICATION GUIDE

### PSALM 91

**What God said to me:**

_____

_____

_____

_____

_____

_____

**What I said to God:**

_____

_____

_____

_____

_____

_____

when He kept His promises to you? ❏ Yes  ❏ No  If so, describe it below and praise Him for being a promise-keeping God.

_____

_Yahweh:_

_I will say of the Lord, "He is my refuge and my fortress, my God in whom I trust" (Ps. 91:2)._

The term _LORD_, written in capital letters, reveals the personal name of God—_Yahweh_ or _Jehovah_. (The word _Lord_ in lowercase letters signifies _Adonai_—the master, the person with authority.) _Yahweh_ signifies the God who is with you all the time. God used this name to reveal Himself to Moses in Exodus 3. When God said to Moses, " 'I AM WHO I AM,' " He was probably saying, in effect, "Go and do what you are told, for I am with you" (see Ex. 3:14).

**Think about a time when you experienced the characteristic of God revealed by the name _Yahweh_. Have you been aware of His presence when you believed that He was asking you to do something difficult?** ❏ Yes  ❏ No  **If so, describe your experience below. Stop and pray, praising God for being _Yahweh_ in your life.**

_____

_Elohim:_

"My God in whom I trust" (Ps. 91:2) reveals the name _Elohim_. It first appears in Genesis 1:1 in the creation story, referring to the strong, covenant-keeping God who is the Creator. Do you regularly approach God as the Creator and worship Him?

**Think about a time when you experienced the characteristic of God revealed by the name _Elohim_. When have you been aware of Him as the One who gave you life and created everything around you? Describe your experience below. Then stop and worship God as the Creator.**

_____

Other names of God also help you focus on who He is and enable you to praise Him. Consider these:
- _Jehovah Jireh_—the God who provides
- _Jehovah Shalom_—the God who brings peace
- _Jehovah Sabaoth_—the God who brings spiritual help
- _Jehovah Rapha_—the God who heals

You may want to use a Bible dictionary to examine some of the names of God. Understanding the characteristics of God will help you know how to praise Him. God's names are revealed in your experiences with Him. Let Him reveal Himself to you as you worship Him.

REASONS TO PRAISE GOD

As you practice praying in faith, consider these other reasons God is worthy of praise. You can praise Him because—

- *He is the living God.* Matthew 16:16 states Simon Peter's answer when Jesus asked who He is: " 'You are the Christ, the Son of the living God.' "
- *He is holy.* As people entered the temple area, they were aware of God's holiness. Psalm 29:2 says, "Worship the Lord in the splendor of his holiness."
- *He is spirit.* He is not material form but the highest form of existence. God's spirit form allows Him to be with people everywhere:

> *Where can I go from your Spirit?*
> *Where can I flee from your presence? (Ps. 139:7)*

- *He is love.* The primary purpose behind His revelation is love (see John 3:16).
- *He is Father.* He is the Father of our Lord Jesus Christ, whose death allows us to enter the Father's presence: " 'No one comes to the Father except through me' " (John 14:6).
- *He is glory.* The word glory refers to His influence and importance in the universe. Hebrews 1:3 says, "The Son is the radiance of God's glory and the exact representation of his being, sustaining all things by his powerful word."

Praise God because of who He is, not because of what He does. Praise is pure worship and adoration. In praise you affirm God and express your love for Him.

**Stop and pray. Review the list of reasons God is worthy of your praise. Use each one to praise Him as you continue to develop the discipline of praying in faith.**

I hope that by now you have seen growth in your life because of prayer—both praying alone during your quiet time and praying with your prayer partner. In your prayer time I hope that God has begun to reveal to you persons who are not Christians for whom you need to pray. One way to begin building a witnessing relationship is to show God's love to someone who is not a Christian. In the process of befriending that person, pave the way for sharing the gospel.

My family once lived across the street from a nice couple, who often asked our children to work for them. Although we became friends, this

**Understanding the characteristics of God will help you know how to praise Him.**

**Praise God because of who He is, not because of what He does.**

couple did not respond positively to a gospel witness. During the Christmas season I took a poinsettia to them. Soon the woman came over and asked if I would pray for her. She had obviously been drinking. Later, I was able to lead her to receive Christ. The act of giving the plant paved the way for me to witness. I was thankful that God had led me to prepare the way for the woman to receive the gospel.

 This week show God's love to a non-Christian by doing something kind for that person. Afterward, describe here what you did and the person's response.

_____

_____

 In the margin write this week's memory verse, John 15:7. Below the verse describe how you feel about beginning or developing the practice of praying in faith.

# DAY 4

## *The Altar of Confession*

After you have thanked God for what He has done and have praised Him for who He is, confess your sins to Him. In addition to glorifying and honoring God, you must also ask God to examine your heart.

### THE NEED TO CONFESS SIN

Earlier this week you read about the prophet Isaiah's experience when he saw God and witnessed His glory. As this occurred, Isaiah also became aware of the contrast between God's holiness and his own sinfulness.

**Read Isaiah 6:4-6 in the margin and complete this sentence:**

**When Isaiah experienced the Lord's glory, he _____ his sin.**

When you approach God's throne and become aware of His presence, your personal sin confronts you and weighs heavy on your mind. After such a divine confrontation it is appropriate to confess your sin, just as Isaiah did when he experienced God's glory.

Before the death of Christ, people offered sacrifices in an effort to

*"At the sound of their voices the doorposts and thresholds shook and the temple was filled with smoke. 'Woe to me!' I cried. 'I am ruined! For I am a man of unclean lips, and I live among a people of unclean lips, and my eyes have seen the King, the Lord Almighty' " (Isa. 6:4-6).*

atone for their sins. They sacrificed blood offerings on an altar. Today no animal offering is required for you to atone for your sins. Christ offered Himself as a sacrifice for you so that your sins may be forgiven. First John 1:8-10, in the margin, says that when you confess your sins to the Father, He is faithful to forgive you.

In confession you let God examine your heart, and He shows you what separates you from Him—the barriers that keep you from experiencing Him to the fullest. Full fellowship with the Father is blocked if your life contains unconfessed sin. The beautiful words of Psalm 139 illustrate the proper attitude about confession. Read verses 23-24 in the margin. The psalmist displays an attitude of openness by asking God to make him aware of his unrighteousness so that he can grow. The Holy Spirit's job is to convict us of things that offend our holy God. You do not have to guess what might be sin in your life. If you open yourself to His leading, the Holy Spirit will show you things that offend God.

**Reread 1 John 1:8-10 in the margin. According to this passage, why do you need to confess the sin in your life?**
❑ **The Father will forgive you and cleanse you.**
❑ **You deceive yourself and do not live in the truth if you claim to be above sin.**
❑ **The Father can show that He is faithful to His promise to forgive you when you confess sin.**
❑ **So that you will feel better.**

The Father wants you to confess sin so that He can do what He has promised to do: forgive you and cleanse you. You fool only yourself when you claim to be sinless. The Father to whom you pray knows the sin in your heart. Confessing sin makes you feel better, but that is not the purpose. The purpose is to restore your fellowship with God. All of the answers except the last one are reasons for confessing sin.

Furthermore, as Psalm 66:18 reveals, God does not listen to your prayers if you continue to cling to your unrighteous ways, refusing to acknowledge and confess them. Confessing sin in your life is a crucial next step in your fellowship with the Father through prayer.

 **In your quiet time today read Psalm 51, David's confession. After you have read this passage, complete the Daily Master Communication Guide on page 66. Do this before you read further.**

## WHAT DO YOU NEED TO CONFESS?

As you study about confession and ask the Lord to search your heart, a good passage to read is Ephesians 4:22-32. In this passage Paul addressed the church, but his admonitions apply in all relationships and to all behavior.

*"If we claim to be without sin, we deceive ourselves and the truth is not in us. If we confess our sins, he is faithful and just and will forgive us our sins and purify us from all unrighteousness. If we claim we have not sinned, we make him out to be a liar and his word has no place in our lives"* (1 John 1:8-10).

*Search me, O God, and know my heart;*
    *test me and know my anxious thoughts.*
*See if there is any offensive way in me,*
    *and lead me in the way everlasting* (Ps. 139:23-24).

*If I had cherished sin in my heart,*
    *the Lord would not have listened* (Ps. 66:18).

## DAILY MASTER COMMUNICATION GUIDE

### PSALM 51

**What God said to me:**

_____

_____

_____

_____

_____

_____

**What I said to God:**

_____

_____

_____

_____

_____

_____

Read Ephesians 4:22-32 and ask yourself, _What do I need to confess?_ As you open yourself to the Lord, ask Him to point out what is not right in your life and to help you confess it.

_You were taught, with regard to your former way of life, to put off your old self, which is being corrupted by its deceitful desires; to be made new in the attitude of your minds; and to put on the new self, created to be like God in true righteousness and holiness. Therefore each of you must put off falsehood and speak truthfully to his neighbor, for we are all members of one body. In your anger do not sin: Do not let the sun go down while you are still angry, and do not give the devil a foothold. He who has been stealing must steal no longer, but must work, doing something useful with his own hands, that he may have something to share with those in need. Do not let any unwholesome talk come out of your mouths, but only what is helpful for building others up according to their needs, that it may benefit those who listen. And do not grieve the Holy Spirit of God, with whom you were sealed for the day of redemption. Get rid of all bitterness, rage and anger, brawling and slander, along with every form of malice. Be kind and compassionate to one another, forgiving each other, just as in Christ God forgave you (Eph. 4:22-32)._

**Check anything of which the Lord convicted you:**

❑ deceitful desires    ❑ brawling
❑ falsehood           ❑ laziness
❑ anger               ❑ slander
❑ bitterness          ❑ unwholesome talk
❑ rage                ❑ malice
❑ stealing

**Now write a confession in which you ask God to forgive you of the matter or matters you checked.**

_____

_____

_____

_____

Confession is an important part of maintaining a right relationship with God. Maturity in discipleship can be thought of as the degree to which you experience harmony, or wholeness, in relating to God and others. You experience this harmony when you have regular fellowship with Christ, that is, a daily pattern of praying in faith. That is why praying in faith is a major component of your lifelong, obedient relationship with Him.

LEARNING THE DISCIPLE'S CROSS

**To summarize what you are learning about praying in faith, draw the portions of the Disciple's Cross you have studied. Draw a circle with Christ, the lower crossbar with Word written on it, and the accompanying Scriptures. Then draw the upper crossbar with prayer written on it. Under prayer write John 15:7, the verse that accompanies this discipline. Explain the cross aloud as you draw these parts. Be prepared to explain it at your next group session.**

**Maturity in discipleship can be thought of as the degree to which you experience harmony, or wholeness, in relating to God and others.**

**Continue memorizing John 15:7. Say this verse aloud to a family member or a friend. You may want to call one of your *MasterLife* group members for whom you are praying and to practice saying the verse to him or her as you remind the person of your prayers.**

How are you progressing with your Prayer-Covenant List? Are you making notes of prayers as you see them answered? You may find it helpful to set aside a period of time every few weeks to study your Prayer-Covenant List and to praise God for answered prayers. You could do this as you travel by yourself on a lengthy trip. You could take it to a nearby park for time with the Lord. You could get up early one morning to examine it. I try to do this at least once a week. Then every month I go back over all of the requests to observe what God has done. I am constantly amazed that God answers so many of my prayers. As I read my prayer journal and prayer requests, God shows me how faithful He has been. Usually, not every request has been answered, but He teaches me to walk in faith by answering many of them.

↑ **Spend time on your Prayer-Covenant List. Pray for the prayer needs on it. Then decide on a time during the next week when you will study what God is doing in your life. Write the day and time here: _____.**

# DAY 5

## *In God's Presence*

**N**ow you find yourself in the presence of God. This is a holy place. The Father wants you to approach Him with your needs. He waits to grant what you ask that is in His will. He delights in doing so. Now that you have thanked Him for your blessings, have given Him the praise He is due, and have confessed your sins, you are ready to talk with Him about needs, both yours and others'.

### BRINGING YOUR NEEDS TO GOD

When you think about praying for needs, you can think of the place in the temple called the holy of holies, the temple's most sacred area. In Bible times only the high priest had access to this innermost chamber. Because of Jesus Christ, however, you have access to God and can approach Him in all His holiness with the deepest needs of your heart. You can approach the innermost part of the very sanctuary of God. In that holy of holies everything is laid bare before Him, as the verse in the margin reveals.

↑ **In your quiet time today read Hebrews 4, which states that Jesus Christ is the only high priest you need. After you have read this passage, complete the Daily Master Communication Guide on page 71.**

In the chapter you read, Hebrews 4:14-16, in the margin on the next page, states that Jesus, as our Great High Priest, understands our needs.

**How does Hebrews 4:14-16 tell you that you are to approach God's throne of grace?**
**With**_____

---

*"Nothing in all creation is hidden from God's sight. Everything is uncovered and laid bare before the eyes of him to whom we must give account"* (Heb. 4:13).

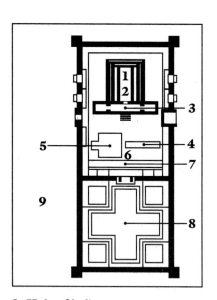

1. Holy of holies
2. Holy place
3. Porch
4. Slaughterhouse
5. Altar
6. Court of priests
7. Court of Israel
8. Court of women
9. Court of Gentiles

You can approach God's throne of grace with confidence because, as the Scripture says, He is ready to grant you mercy and grace to help you in your time of need. He is pleased to hear your personal requests. How do you know that Jesus wants you to pray freely about your needs? Your memory verse for this week ensures it.

As you think about the marvelous promise in your Scripture-memory verse, John 15:7, say the verse aloud again. As you say it, think about a loving God who finds your requests pleasing to His ears.

## PRAYING FOR YOURSELF

Today you will study two types of requests: petition and intercession. Petition is asking for yourself. You know that God encourages people to pray for their personal concerns, because His Word is filled with answered requests. For example, Luke 1:13 contains God's response to Zechariah's petition for a son. His request was answered with the birth of John the Baptist.

God's answers to your prayers help mold you into the person He wants you to become. He does not grant petitions that you pray for the wrong reason or that He knows would bring the wrong outcome in your life. Read 1 John 5:14-15 in the margin.

**List personal needs for which you desire to pray. Use the following categories to prompt your thinking, but do not limit your list to these or feel that you must write a request for each one. You may need to use extra paper to expand your list.**

**Christ-honoring relationships with others:** _____

_____

**The ability to manage my time wisely:** _____

_____

**Concerns on my job:** _____

_____

**My ministry at church:** _____

_____

**Guidance in my vocation:** _____

_____

*"Since we have a great high priest who has gone through the heavens, Jesus the Son of God, let us hold firmly to the faith we profess. For we do not have a high priest who is unable to sympathize with our weaknesses, but we have one who has been tempted in every way, just as we are—yet was without sin. Let us then approach the throne of grace with confidence, so that we may receive mercy and find grace to help us in our time of need"* (Heb. 4:14-16).

*"This is the confidence we have in approaching God: that if we ask anything according to his will, he hears us"* (1 John 5: 14-15).

Physical and emotional health: _____

_____

Ability to resist temptation: _____

_____

Material needs: _____

_____

*"Confess your sins to each other and pray for each other so that you may be healed. The prayer of a righteous man is powerful and effective" (Jas. 5:16).*

*" 'Holy Father, protect them by the power of your name—the name you gave me—so that they may be one as we are one. My prayer is not that you take them out of the world but that you protect them from the evil one. Sanctify them by the truth; your word is truth' " (John 17:11,15,17).*

**God uses you as His vehicle to accomplish His will when you pray for others.**

**Now stop and pray about some of these requests. Pray for God's will in the outcomes of these situations and concerns.**

PRAYING FOR OTHERS
The second type of prayer for needs is intercession—prayer for others. The Bible instructs us to pray for one another, as James 5:16, in the margin, indicates. Jesus prayed for His disciples many times. One of the best examples is found in John 17, in which Jesus prayed for His disciples before He went to the cross. A portion of that prayer appears in the margin. You pray for others for the same reason you pray for yourself: so that God can mold them into the persons He wants them to become. God uses you as His vehicle to accomplish His will when you pray for others.

**How important to you is intercession for others? Check the answer that describes you.**
❑ I am too busy taking care of my own needs to pray for others.
❑ I intercede for others after I handle other areas of ministry.
❑ I intercede for others only in extreme crises, such as when someone is critically ill.
❑ Interceding for others is highly important to me because God can use my intercession to accomplish His will.

**Stop and pray, asking the Father to make you a more fervent intercessor for others.**

As you have kept your Prayer-Covenant List for the past several weeks, you have been interceding for others. By lifting your concerns to Him, you have been an instrument God has used to accomplish His will in the lives of others. Now is a good time to review some of those prayers of intercession.

**List two persons on your Prayer-Covenant List and their needs. Describe ways God has answered your prayers for these individu-**

als. Even if you have seen only partial or incremental answers, list those below. Then pray, thanking God for hearing your prayers. Ask Him to continue to work His will in the lives of those individuals.

| Name | Request | Answer |
|------|---------|--------|
| _____ | _____ | _____ |
| _____ | _____ | _____ |

To review, list the two types of prayers for needs you have studied today. Look back if you need to refresh your memory.

Praying for yourself: _____

Praying for others: _____

For several weeks you have practiced a daily quiet time. Even if you have struggled with it, find someone with whom you can share your testimony about having a daily quiet time. Share with someone who needs to develop this practice or with a friend. This will strengthen your resolve for having a quiet time.

## HAS THIS WEEK MADE A DIFFERENCE?

**Review "My Walk with the Master This Week" at the beginning of this week's material. Mark the activities you have finished by drawing vertical lines in the diamonds beside them. Finish any incomplete activities. Think about what you will say during your group session about your work on these activities.**

As you complete your study of "Pray in Faith," reflect on the experiences you have had this week.
- Have you been praying in faith this week?
- Is having a quiet time becoming a regular part of your life?
- Are you keeping a Prayer-Covenant List and making notes of answers to prayer?

Through this week's work I hope that you have become more aware of how praying in faith helps you develop the disciplines of a disciple and contributes to your lifelong, obedient relationship with Christ. Jesus' purpose in teaching His disciples how to pray was to teach them how to know the Father through prayer. Have you come to know more about the Father through this week's study? Where do you stand now in terms of your lifelong, obedient relationship with Him? Congratulations on taking these important steps. Learning to pray the way Christ wants you to is not easy. It requires that you set aside a self-centered way of life and

**DAILY MASTER COMMUNICATION GUIDE**

**HEBREWS 4**

What God said to me:

_____

_____

_____

_____

_____

_____

_____

What I said to God:

_____

_____

_____

_____

_____

_____

_____

_____

**Starting your prayers with thanksgiving, praise, and confession before making requests means that you have Someone besides yourself at the center of your life.**

look for His will for you instead of your will for yourself. Starting your prayers with thanksgiving, praise, and confession before making requests means that you have Someone besides yourself at the center of your life.

Throughout *MasterLife* you will continue to learn how to pray in faith. When you study book 3, you will see the fullness of all God wants to do in your life through prayer. Following Jesus means that you seek to know and do His will, not just coast through life. By now in *Master-Life* you have seen the sacrifices you need to make in order to walk with the Master and to live in Him. I affirm your willingness to make these sacrifices in order to grow as a disciple of Christ.

# WEEK 4

## Fellowship with Believers

### This Week's Goal
You will experience growth in Christ through relationships in His body.

### My Walk with the Master This Week
You will complete the following activities to develop the six biblical disciplines. When you have completed each activity, draw a vertical line in the diamond beside it.

SPEND TIME WITH THE MASTER
◇ Have a daily quiet time. Check the box beside each day you have a quiet time this week: ❑ Sunday ❑ Monday ❑ Tuesday ❑ Wednesday ❑ Thursday ❑ Friday ❑ Saturday

LIVE IN THE WORD
◇ Read your Bible every day. Write what God says to you and what you say to God.
◇ Memorize John 13:34-35.
◇ Review Luke 9:23, John 15:5, John 8:31-32, and John 15:7.

PRAY IN FAITH
◇ Pray with your prayer partner.
◇ Pray about your priorities and your use of time.
◇ Add requests to your Prayer-Covenant List.

FELLOWSHIP WITH BELIEVERS
◇ Befriend someone in the church who is not a close friend or is not in your *MasterLife* group.

WITNESS TO THE WORLD
◇ Plan your time, using "How to Use MasterTime" and the MasterTime form.
◇ Read "Redeeming the Time" and underline portions that apply to you.

MINISTER TO OTHERS
◇ Continue learning the Disciple's Cross. Explain the meaning of the right crossbar to add to the information about the circle and the vertical crossbar that you learned in previous weeks. Learn the Scriptures that go with each part of the cross.

### This Week's Scripture-Memory Verses
*" 'A new command I give you: Love one another. As I have loved you, so you must love one another. By this all men will know that you are my disciples, if you love one another' " (John 13:34-35).*

# DAY 1

## *The Mark of a Disciple*

When missionary Bruce Schmidt was negotiating to buy three acres of land in a Ugandan valley to begin a new work among unreached people, he found himself face to face with a leader of the Karamojong, one of the most feared tribes in East Africa. "Why are you here, and what do you want?" the chief demanded.

Bruce replied that he was in the valley because of two great things: the Great Commission, which he explained, and the Great Commandment. "In the Great Commandment Jesus said that we are to love God first and to love our neighbor as ourselves. I want to be your neighbor."

To Bruce's surprise, the Karamojong leader voiced no objection. Instead, he appeared to be moved by Bruce's remarks. "Nobody wants to be the neighbor of the Karamojong. We are the most despised tribe in Uganda. All of our neighboring tribes have had their cattle stolen, their women raped, and their men murdered. We can't believe you want to be our neighbor!" the man exclaimed.

By the time the meeting ended, God had melted hearts of stone. This feared Karamojong tribe ultimately gave Bruce and his coworkers 30 acres of land for their new mission work—all because of neighborly love that Bruce extended in Jesus Christ. Although most of us are not placed in a foreign land with hostile tribes as neighbors, we often face hostility as Christians in an evil world. Like Bruce, we are to love our neighbors.

### LOVING ONE ANOTHER

Jesus never intended for you to operate in a vacuum. You cannot be a balanced Christian if you neglect loving relationships with others. If you try to live apart from the fellowship of other believers—the church, which is Christ's body—you will not experience fullness of life in Christ. The Lord put us in a body of believers because sustaining life outside the body is difficult. As we stay connected to people in fellowship and as we love one another, we gain strength from one another.

> **As we stay connected to people in fellowship and as we love one another, we gain strength from one another.**

 **Read this week's Scripture-memory verses, John 13:34-35, in the margin. What did Jesus say identifies His disciples?**

_____

**Now go back and read John 13:34-35 aloud from one to three times to begin memorizing these verses.**

Jesus said that one identifying mark of a disciple is your love for others. Love shows the world that you are His disciple. Loving others and

> " 'A new command I give you: Love one another. As I have loved you, so you must love one another. By this all men will know that you are my disciples, if you love one another' " (John 13:34-35).

being involved in harmonious fellowship with them show that Christ is at the center of your life. Loving relationships are at the very heart of life in Christ. He shows you Himself through fellowship with others. Jesus did not tell His followers to go it alone but to demonstrate the love He modeled for them. You do this in fellowship with other believers.

**Read the following case studies.**

Martha loved the outdoors and enjoyed long walks in the woods. Although Martha was a Christian, she did not attend church, reciting an excuse many people use: "I can worship God better when I'm enjoying His creation." Members of a Bible-study group invited her to attend, but Martha chose to pursue her outdoor interests instead.

Joe had given his life to Christ several years ago but had never become involved in a church. Even though members of a church in his neighborhood visited him, Joe declined to attend. A shy person, Joe could not imagine himself conversing with strangers.

**Underline the excuses Martha and Joe used for declining to fellowship with believers. What kinds of activities do you choose to do instead of fellowship with believers? List them.**

_____

Exploring God's creation is a wonderful way to be aware of His blessings and glory, but it does not take the place of the fellowship Christ intended for you to have with other believers. Shyness around others is a painful matter for some people, but the Father can give you strength to overcome weaknesses so that you can be part of the body. When you have life in Christ and abide in Him, you follow His commands. John 15:12 says, " 'My command is this: Love each other as I have loved you.' "

**Why does John 15:12 say that you are to love other persons?**

_____

John 15:12 says that you are to love other persons because Christ commanded it. Love flows from God through Christ to humankind. Having modeled love for you, Christ commands you to exhibit it to others. Shutting yourself off from the fellowship of others impairs your ability to show love to others and prevents their exhibiting love to you. Your local church represents the body of Christ, in which you can fellowship with other believers. Hebrews 10:24-25, in the margin, clearly teaches that we are to meet together with other believers.

**Love shows the world that you are His disciple.**

_"Let us consider how we may spur one another on toward love and good deeds. Let us not give up meeting together, as some are in the habit of doing, but let us encourage one another—and all the more as you see the Day approaching"_ (Heb. 10:24-25).

*"Each one should use whatever gift he has received to serve others, faithfully administering God's grace in its various forms" (1 Pet. 4:10).*

*" 'As the Father has loved me, so have I loved you. Now remain in my love' " (John 15:9).*

Isolation and individualism are not Christ's ways. Christ brings believers together as a family. We should encourage our fellow Christians to express love for one another. Worshiping together is one way we gain strength and motivation from other disciples. As the verse from 1 Peter in the margin indicates, Christians are to be part of a body of believers, using their gifts to serve others and receiving instruction from God's Word. Anyone who professes to be a Christian but does not attend church is disregarding God's Word and is living outside His will.

The abundant love God the Father has for His Son, Jesus Christ, is the source of the love the Son has for His followers. It is also the model for the love you are to have for others. The depths of Jesus' love, which led Him to the cross, should not surprise you, because it is modeled in the love the Father has for the Son. Read John 15:9 in the margin.

## LEARNING THE DISCIPLE'S CROSS

The fourth discipline of a disciple's life, then, is fellowshipping with believers. You will study this discipline this week as you continue to learn and add to the Disciple's Cross. While the vertical crossbar you have studied for the past two weeks emphasizes your relationship with Christ through the Word and prayer, the horizontal crossbar you will study this week and in week 5 stresses the importance of your relationship with others through fellowship and witness.

Draw the portions of the Disciple's Cross you have studied. Draw a circle with *Christ* in the center and draw the lower crossbar with *Word* written on it. Then draw the upper crossbar with *prayer* written on it. Add the verses that apply. Now draw the right crossbar and write *fellowship* on it. Under *fellowship* write *John 13:34-35*, the verses that accompany it. Refer to the completed cross on page 136 if you need help.

✝ Continue reading your Bible daily during your quiet time. Today read 1 Corinthians 12:12-31, which depicts the special relationship between you and other Christians. After you have read this passage, complete the Daily Master Communication Guide in the margin.

## DAY 2

# *The Gift of Accountability*

God has shown me many times that I can do nothing without the fellowship of believers in the body of Christ. When I was in college, my friends and I decided to conduct a huge youth revival in my friend's hometown of Borger, Texas. We secured the high-school auditorium, put up huge billboards, announced the event on the radio, and delivered posters to stores. But at the last minute high-school officials told us that church leaders in the community—members of our own denomination—had pressured the school not to let us use the facility. Because we had not sought the local churches' involvement in advance, our plan was backfiring.

I prayed, "Lord, You cannot let us down after we have done so much to prepare," but He taught us another lesson: that we could do nothing without Him. We had undertaken this task on our own for God rather than asking what He wanted. We had talked and prayed about the revival but had then gone ahead with our plans.

This experience was a crushing defeat but a lesson well learned. We left town, convinced that we would not again try to do anything without God's direct leadership and without working within the framework of the local church.

**Have you ever had a disappointing experience in Christian service because you were working outside the fellowship of believers? ❏ Yes ❏ No If so, describe your experience.**

_____

_____

My friends and I had not first prayed in faith for God's direction before we proceeded. We had not asked God to search our hearts to determine whether selfish motives and desires for success were driving our plans. We had not sought the local churches' support. We had failed to live as part of the body of Christ.

---

**DAILY MASTER COMMUNICATION GUIDE**

1 CORINTHIANS 12:12-31

**What God said to me:**

_____

_____

_____

_____

_____

_____

**What I said to God:**

_____

_____

_____

_____

_____

_____

_____

Say aloud your memory verses for the week. Write what these verses say about the importance of fellowshipping with Christ's people.

_____

_____

You may have answered something like this: I may be obedient to Christ in a number of ways, but unless I demonstrate love for His people, I do not show that I am His disciple.

## GOD WORKS THROUGH OTHERS

**Many times God reveals Himself through the individuals He places in your path.**

Many times God reveals Himself through the individuals He places in your path. Life in Christ includes trying to live in fellowship with your brothers and sisters. Often through that fellowship others speak a God-anointed word to you that helps you see a problem more clearly or make the right decision. Christian friends can help hold you accountable for times when you get off course. They can remind you of what the Word says. They can lovingly help you recognize your misplaced priorities. The Father works through others in the church to accomplish His will in your life.

Read these case studies and answer the questions that follow.

> Anita and her grown daughter had not spoken in years. Anita longed to make relations right between them. She invited her daughter home for a special weekend to attempt to repair their relationship. Anita spent every spare moment of the weekend cooking food for her daughter and buying her presents, hoping these actions would make her daughter want to be close to her. She also asked her friends at church to pray for them.

How could Anita's friends at church show love for her?

_____

_____

> Charles worked two jobs to provide income for his family. He was away from home so much that he was seldom available to his wife and children. His children wanted him to attend their sports games and school events, but Charles had to miss most of them. He managed to take his family to church about twice a month.

How could fellowship with other believers help Charles?

In Anita's story you may have noted that Christian friends could have visited with Anita and prayed with her about her daughter. Without necessarily giving her advice, they could have helped Anita examine her choices. What had she done to make things right? Had Anita apologized to her daughter for any wrong on her part? Had she discussed the situation with her pastor or with a Christian counselor? Christian friends could invite Anita to church activities to give her other focuses in her life. They could lovingly model ways she could connect with the Vine as the source of help.

For Charles's situation you may have replied that Christian friends could help with his employment situation. They could help him network among church members to find a job with better pay, which would eliminate the need for two jobs. They could invite him to family activities planned by the church to provide opportunities for him to be with his children in a church setting. Men could include him in their accountability-and-support group. They could lovingly help Charles see his children's need for him and could help him connect with the Vine as the source of power.

## AN INSTRUMENT OF CHRIST'S LOVE

If you want to be Jesus' true disciple and to have a personal, lifelong, obedient relationship with Him, you will show love for others by fellowshipping with them and by being Christ's instrument in their lives. Christ's love can flow through you to them. You can help them be all Christ wants them to be. The right crossbar of fellowship on the Disciple's Cross reminds you of the importance of your relationships with others.

 Say aloud your Scripture-memory verses for this week, John 13:34-35. Say them to your prayer partner in your prayer time this week.

 Read 1 Corinthians 12:31—13:13 during your quiet time. Let God speak to you through this passage about loving one another. After reading this passage, complete the Daily Master Communication Guide in the margin.

---

### DAILY MASTER COMMUNICATION GUIDE

1 CORINTHIANS 12:31—13:13

**What God said to me:**

_____

_____

_____

_____

_____

_____

**What I said to God:**

_____

_____

_____

_____

_____

_____

_____

# DAY 3

## *Help for Withered Christians*

**Fellowship with other Christians is also crucial to avoid withering in your Christian life.**

Fellowship with other Christians is also crucial to avoid withering in your Christian life. Roy Edgemon, my longtime colleague and one of the "three men at the gate" who encouraged me to bring *MasterLife* to the United States, recalls a time when the fellowship of other Christians—the aspect of the Disciple's Cross you are studying this week—helped revive him in the midst of spiritual withering.

As a busy pastor in Texas, Roy was almost burned out from church building programs and heavy involvement in state denominational leadership. One night a missionary from Africa named Bud Frey conducted a rally at Roy's church in Odessa, Texas. As Frey described a recent period of spiritual withering and exhaustion, "I could tell he had been in the same shape I was in," Roy said. Frey said a Christian friend admonished him, "You're a Bud Frey cause, not a Jesus cause." The friend urged him to "find out how the Lord needs to have His way with you." Frey said he began learning how to be a Jesus cause, changing his lifestyle to ensure a daily quiet time and a more personal relationship with Christ.

Roy took out a slip of paper, wrote a note, and passed it down the aisle to Frey. The note said, "If you know how I can stop this world long enough to get off, I want to talk to you." But to Roy's embarrassment, before the note could make its way down the aisle to Frey, a friend, Bill Hogue, read the message and wrote under Roy's comment, "Me too."

"I didn't want anyone to know I was in that kind of shape," said Roy. But Roy, Bill Hogue, and their wives spent most of the remainder of the night talking and praying with Bud Frey. The meeting resulted in life change for Roy, he said.

"I started getting up in the morning and praying regularly," Roy recalls. "Before, if we didn't have decisions in every service, I had taken it as a personal defeat. I was doing the Lord's work but wasn't letting the Lord work through me." Fellowship with other Christians who shared their own brokenness helped encourage and restore this pastor to a life of usefulness in God's kingdom.

**Has fellowship with a Christian friend ever helped you when you were withering spiritually and were not experiencing a victorious life in Christ? ❑ Yes ❑ No  If so, describe this experience.**

_____

_____

Read 2 Timothy 1:1-14, which depicts the special relationship between Paul and Timothy, during your quiet time today. After you have read this passage, complete the Daily Master Communication Guide in the margin.

## A NETWORK OF SUPPORT

You can also encourage others as you become an instrument of Christ. What happens to your fellow church members is important to you. First Corinthians 12:27 says, "You are the body of Christ, and each one of you is a part of it." If one member of the body withers—experiences illness, loss, or a diminished spiritual life—the entire body suffers, including you. The body cares for each member of the body so that together all of the members become more complete in Christ's love.

Fellowship among Christians can span the globe, thanks to modern technological methods such as electronic mail. One of my colleagues at work regularly uses electronic mail to encourage a pastor in another state who is experiencing interpersonal challenges in his congregation. This fellowship across the miles and computer networks can help remedy the isolation and loneliness of pastors who sometimes feel that they have few confidantes in their communities. Christians urgently need fellowship with other believers.

## SHARING WHAT GOD IS DOING

God may want you to help build up the body by sharing what He is doing in your life. Have you shared with other believers ways you are growing in Christ as you learn what being His disciple means? You can tell others about your experiences of praying in faith, memorizing Scripture, or a daily quiet time. Sharing your experiences may lead another person to seek a closer relationship with the Lord.

As you work today on this week's Scripture-memory verses, John 13:34-35, tell someone how you have grown in Christ from the practice of memorizing Scripture.

**Stop and pray, asking God to show you how He wants you to work within the body of Christ to encourage others.**

---

### DAILY MASTER COMMUNICATION GUIDE

2 TIMOTHY 1:1-14

**What God said to me:**

_____

_____

_____

_____

_____

_____

**What I said to God:**

_____

_____

_____

_____

_____

_____

_____

# DAY 4

## *What Christ Expects*

*" 'As the Father has loved me, so have I loved you. My command is this: Love each other as I have loved you. Greater love has no one than this, that he lay down his life for his friends' " (John 15:9,12-13).*

**W**hen disciples fellowship with other believers, they take care to develop Christ-honoring relationships with others. Relationships do not just happen. They require careful cultivation and nurture. Because all of us have sinful natures, we can fall into patterns of thoughtlessness in the way we treat others. Hatred, snobbery, jealousy, and backbiting have no place in the life of a follower of Christ. The Scriptures instruct us about how Christ expects us to treat others with whom we fellowship.

FRIENDSHIP: A HIGH PRIORITY
**Read John 15:9,12-13 in the margin.**

**Why are you to love other persons?**

_____

*A friend loves at all times, and a brother is born for adversity (Prov. 17:17).*

**At the heart of friendship is the willingness to _____ _____ if necessary.**

You should love other persons because of the love that flows from God through Christ to you. Jesus put so much value on friendship and fellowship that He said friends should be willing even to give their lives for one another if necessary. Jesus made friendship a high priority! Jesus laid down His life for others, and later, some of His disciples did, too. Fellowshipping with other believers and loving those believers with the kind of sacrificial love that Jesus demonstrated are important parts of life in Christ and of a lifelong, obedient relationship with Him.

*" 'If your brother sins against you, go and show him his fault, just between the two of you. If he listens to you, you have won your brother over. But if he will not listen, take one or two others along, so that every matter may be established by the testimony of two or three witnesses' " (Matt. 18:15).*

*"Brothers, do not slander one another. Anyone who speaks against his brother or judges him speaks against the law and judges it" (Jas. 4:11).*

*"We proclaim to you what we have seen and heard, so that you also may have fellowship with us. And our fellowship is with the Father and with his Son, Jesus Christ" (1 John 1:3).*

**Examine what the Bible says about the way friends are to act toward one another. Read the verses in the margin. Then match each reference in the left column with the correct statement in the right column.**

___ 1. Proverbs 17:17    a. **Friends care enough to confront one another in love if necessary.**

___ 2. Matthew 18:15    b. **Friends do not gossip or make hurtful remarks about one another.**

___ 3. James 4:11    c. **Friends want the best for one another and therefore present the gospel to friends who do not know Christ.**

___ 4. 1 John 1:3    d. **Friends love one another regardless of the situations they face.**

Now review the statements in the right column that describe characteristics of friendship. Draw a star beside the trait or traits that represent the biggest challenges in your friendships. Stop and pray that God will change you in these areas through Christ's love.

Was one of the statements you checked item a—caring enough to confront? People sometimes struggle with this issue, believing that confronting a friend is not Christlike because it seems to call for hostility. Actually, confronting a friend in love is a very caring act. Sometimes people tell others that they have a problem with a friend yet never go directly to that person. That type of indirect communication can hurt the relationship. It can also hurt the body of Christ. Disagreements between individuals in a church can escalate, widening their circle to include others. Eventually, small disputes can develop into major rifts that prevent the body of Christ from doing its work.

Jesus was very clear about how Christians are to resolve difficulties face to face. These Bible verses tell you how a follower of Christ relates to others. You can learn loving, diplomatic ways to communicate how you feel so that such communication strengthens and does not harm the relationship. The correct answers to the previous exercise are 1. d, 2. a, 3. b, 4. c. Book 4 discusses more about how to reconcile broken relationships.

THE COST OF NEGLECTING RELATIONSHIPS

Sometimes you may find that you have closed yourself off from persons who care about you. Do you shut out persons rather than get involved in their lives? Do you avoid persons rather than risk cultivating relationships? Because you have been hurt in past friendships perhaps you withdraw rather than make yourself vulnerable again. Even if you attend church, you may not allow friendships to form there. You may think you can attend, listen to the sermon, and then spend the rest of the week avoiding fellow believers who might want to get involved in your life.

**In the previous paragraph underline statements or questions with which you can identify.**

If you avoid fellowshipping with believers because you do not want to risk relationships, you miss opportunities to serve your family in Christ. When difficulties come your way, relationships with other believers can provide resources to meet your needs. The most serious result of neglecting fellowship with believers is that it inevitably creates distance between you and God.

**Read 1 Thessalonians 2:1-13 today during your quiet time. After you have read about Paul's love for and ministry with the Christians at Thessalonica, complete the Daily Master Communication Guide in the margin.**

## DAILY MASTER COMMUNICATION GUIDE

1 THESSALONIANS 2:1-13

**What God said to me:**

_____

_____

_____

_____

_____

_____

_____

_____

**What I said to God:**

_____

_____

_____

_____

_____

_____

_____

_____

Paul's example with the Thessalonians can guide you in relating to your *MasterLife* group members. Likely by now, after four group sessions together, you are forming a special bond with your group members. Although you may not have known some of these persons well before you began studying *MasterLife*, long, enduring friendships can form as a result of this fellowship. You may begin to see in these persons some of the traits of friendship you studied on page 82. Be thankful for the trust, support, and fellowship that have begun to develop.

**Take to heart John 15:12-13, the verses you have read several times this week, and lovingly lift your group members to the Father in prayer. Stop now and pray for each of your *MasterLife* group members by name. Ask God to bless each person through this study. Ask Him to help you be available as a friend to your fellow members.**

USING YOUR TIME EFFECTIVELY
A lack of time is an excuse you may use when you assess why you do not take advantage of—or create—opportunities to fellowship with believers. Perhaps you have already had difficulty finding time to do your daily assignments. For the rest of today and in day 5 you will learn ways to be a better steward of your time.

 **The following suggestions can help you use your time more effectively. As you read them, underline statements that seem relevant to you.**

**When we treat time as a gift from God, we spend our time in ways that are more consistent with His purposes.**

---

**REDEEMING THE TIME**
We search for time and yearn for more. Time has become our most cherished possession. Our world focuses on the race against time, and the clock dictates the tempo of our lives.

**Ask God's Purpose for Our Time**
Time is God's gift to us. The art of having time occurs when we live according to God's purposes. We are responsible to Him for every minute He gives us. If we listen to Him more carefully, our lives are more harmonious. When we treat time as a gift from God, we spend our time in ways that are more consistent with His purposes. We become good stewards of our time. We find that the events of our lives flow together more smoothly and that we have more time to do the things that need to be done.

**Ask God's Direction for the Day**
Time is an opportunity God gives us to discover and carry out His purposes. If we believe that Christ is the Lord of our time, we can believe that He has a design for this day, as well as for our entire lives. Knowing and doing God's will for our lives involves knowing and doing God's will for this day in our lives.

### Prioritize What You Do Before You Do It

The apostle Paul said that wisdom is related to the use of time: "Be very careful, then, how you live—not as unwise but as wise, making the most of every opportunity, because the days are evil" (Eph. 5:15-16). The word translated "making the most of every opportunity" literally means "buying up every chance" or snapping up bargains at a sale. God's time is a priceless commodity. He calls us to invest our opportunities in worthwhile pursuits. The wise use of time means being alert to every opportunity for Christian ministry and witness. Seize the critical moment when it arrives: the chance encounter, the turn in conversation, the unplanned incident. Be prepared, expect such opportunities, and grasp them. Do not miss a chance to do Christ's work at the wise moment!

### Do It in Priority Order, but Leave Yourself Open for God to Redirect You

We experience freedom when we obey God's purposes. Jesus was a truly free but purposeful person living an unhurried life. Jesus had plenty of time to speak to a foreign woman he met at a well, to spend holidays with His disciples, to admire the lilies of the field, to wash His disciples' feet, to answer their naive questions patiently. Most important, He had time to spend a whole night in prayer before an important decision.

A time of quiet meditation is good for our spiritual lives. We rediscover how to take things easily, how to rest as God commanded, how to meditate and pray. In quietness we rediscover the inner peace the world needs. We make a clear distinction between what is really important and what is secondary.

**The wise use of time means being alert to every opportunity for Christian ministry and witness.**

Check the benefits you are receiving from your daily quiet time.

❏ Learning how to take things easily
❏ Learning how to rest as God commanded
❏ Learning how to meditate and pray
❏ Rediscovering inner peace
❏ Learning to distinguish between what is really important and what is secondary

Draw a star beside the above area or areas you still need to work on.

 Continue to memorize this week's Scripture-memory verses, John 13:34-35. Write them in the margin from one to three times. Review the verses you memorized earlier.

## DAY 5

# The Model of Friendship

**F**ellowship was the centerpiece of one of Jesus' last messages to His disciples as He was on the way to the cross. He wanted to tell His most beloved followers all they would need to know to carry on His work after He was no longer on earth physically.

**Read John 15:14-15 in the margin. Underline two things Jesus considered important to communicate to His disciples.**

*" 'You are my friends if you do what I command. I no longer call you servants, because a servant does not know his master's business. Instead, I have called you friends, for everything that I learned from my Father I have made known to you' " (John 15:14-15).*

Jesus wanted the disciples to know that He considered them friends, not servants. Their relationship was that of friends who loved one another in fellowship. He also wanted them to know that He had taught them everything He learned from His Father. Unlike the guarded way someone would treat servants, the Master openly discussed His business with the disciples. Jesus was reminding His disciples that they would have all the knowledge they needed to do His work after He was gone.

Like the disciples, you have all the knowledge you need to do the Father's work. The marching orders for discipleship that Jesus gave His followers are the same orders today for your lifelong, obedient relationship with Christ. Jesus is your friend. He set the model for fellowship, and you as His disciple can act on that model.

**In John 15:16-17, in the margin, underline the three things Jesus wanted to happen in the lives of His disciples.**

*" 'You did not choose me, but I chose you and appointed you to go and bear fruit—fruit that will last. Then the Father will give you whatever you ask in my name. This is my command: Love each other' " (John 15: 16-17).*

This passage emphasizes the high priority Jesus placed on fellowship with believers. He emphasized three reasons He chose the disciples: He appointed them to (1) bear fruit, (2) ask the Father in His name, and (3) love one another. In week 3 you learned about the second of those reasons as you studied praying in faith. You will study more in week 5 about bearing fruit. The third priority, loving one another, is the emphasis of this week's study. Christian love is not the identifying mark of extraordinary disciples—those who go beyond the call of duty. It is the identifying mark of all disciples. Those who obey His commands love one another.

### A STRONG BODY

*" 'My prayer is … that all of them may be one, Father, just as you are in me and I am in you. May they also be in us so that the world may believe that you have sent me. I have given them the glory that you gave me, that they may be one as we are one. May they be brought to complete unity to let the world know that you sent me and have loved them even as you have loved me' " (John 17:20-22).*

The encouragement that springs from fellowship with believers also gives you strength to witness. John 17:20-22, in the margin, describes the complete unity that Christ wants in the body. People who are united in Christ can be effective witnesses for Him. Jesus wanted unity, not division, in the church so that others would believe in Him. A church with members who argue and fail to demonstrate love to one another does not appear to a lost world as if it has something to offer.

Furthermore, believers need one another's encouragement when they try to win others to Christ. Fellow church members can pray for you, encourage you, and help ground you in Scripture as you prepare to share your faith. The church can make you feel useful and supported when you witness to persons who need the Lord.

If you have friends, coworkers, family members, or other acquaintances who do not know Jesus, perhaps you have listed them on your Prayer-Covenant List. Continue to pray in faith that you will seek strength from the body of Christ for witnessing opportunities that the Father puts in your path. Pray that God will give you an opportunity and will help you plan a time to share about your relationship with Christ.

 **Stop now and review your Prayer-Covenant List. Perhaps this day's study has brought other persons or requests to mind. Add them to the list now.**

 **Say aloud your Scripture-memory verses, John 13:34-35, to someone you consider to be a caring friend. Use this as an opportunity to thank this person for his or her friendship.**

 **Again read John 15 in your quiet time today. This time look for teachings about the discipline a Christian needs to fellowship with believers. When you have read this passage, complete the Daily Master Communication Guide in the margin.**

## MOVING BEYOND YOUR COMFORT ZONE

Perhaps fellowshipping with believers is easy for you as long as you are within your comfort zone. You likely have a comfortable circle of friends in your Bible-study group, in your *MasterLife* group, or in another area of your church. But when Christ commands you to love others, He does not put restrictions on those you are to love. Sometimes you may need to reach outside your close circle of friends to extend fellowship.

**Befriend someone in your church or at work who is not in your close circle of friends or in your *MasterLife* group.**

When you think about extending yourself outside your familiar circle, the old protest about time may arise again. You may counter: I barely have time for myself and my family's needs. How can you ask me to take time to get to know someone else? Yesterday you read about redeeming the time to become a better steward of your time. Today you will learn to use a MasterTime form to set your priorities. You will find the MasterTime form on page 138.

Although I like to do things spontaneously, I have learned that in

**DAILY MASTER COMMUNICATION GUIDE**

**JOHN 15**

**What God said to me:**

_____

_____

_____

_____

_____

_____

**What I said to God:**

_____

_____

_____

_____

_____

_____

_____

order to get the priority things done, I must plan my schedule every day, using the MasterTime process. I never get everything I planned to do finished, but at least I know that I have done the priority things. If I do not prioritize my time, others will prioritize it for me.

 **Here are directions for using MasterTime. As you read, underline portions that seem important to you.**

---

**HOW TO USE MASTERTIME**

1. Trust the Lord to direct you in all you do: "Trust in the Lord with all your heart. Never rely on what you think you know. Remember the Lord in everything you do, and he will show you the right way" (Prov. 3:5-6, GNB).
   - Ask God to show you His purposes for you in His kingdom: " 'Seek first his kingdom and his righteousness, and all these things will be given to you as well' " (Matt. 6:33).
   - Make annual, monthly, and weekly lists of the major goals you believe God has given you.

2. Plan your daily work under the Master's leadership: "You may make your plans, but God directs your actions" (Prov. 16:9, GNB).
   - List on the MasterTime form the things you need to do by basic categories. Plan one day or each day for a week, including all areas of your life: God, family, church, and recreation.
   - Write under the "Time" column on the form the amount of time you estimate you need to complete each task. You may prefer to write the time of day you plan to do it, for example, "See Mr. Jones, 9:00–9:30 a.m."
   - Rank the tasks according to your priorities and write that number in the "Priority" column on the form. You may choose to rank only within categories, since you can save time by doing similar tasks in order, such as telephoning. You may also rank them without any regard to category. Minutes spent in planning save hours. Set aside time for planning at the beginning of each day. Ten or 15 minutes will save hours later.

3. "Ask the Lord to bless your plans, and you will be successful in carrying them out" (Prov. 16:3, GNB).

4. Depend on the Lord to direct your actions: "You may make your plans, but God directs your actions" (Prov. 16:9, GNB).
   - Do the tasks in the order planned to save time and to receive immediate direction about the next task to do.
   - When God directs you otherwise, follow His immediate leading. Interruptions and unplanned events are sometimes God's ways to get you to do His will. However, ask His leadership, because Satan can also stop you from doing God's will. Ask yourself:

---

**Plan your daily work under the Master's leadership.**

**Depend on the Lord to direct your actions.**

—Is this one of God's priorities I might not have anticipated?

—Is God trying to teach me something?

—Does He want me to help someone I had not considered?

—Does it contribute to one of my long-range goals? If so, is it a high enough priority to interrupt my list of priorities for today?

—Is it important or merely urgent?

—Is this the best time to do it? Could I do it some other time?

—Can it be delegated to someone else?

—How much do someone else's responsibilities depend on my doing this task at this time?

5. Discipline yourself to carry out your plans: "It is better to win control over yourself than whole cities" (Prov. 16:32, GNB).
   • The key to self-control is Master control.
   • When you fail, do not waste time blaming yourself and feeling guilty. Ask forgiveness and submit yourself to the Master's will.

6. Leave the results to God. "Men cast lots to learn God's will, but God himself determines the answer" (Prov. 16:33, GNB).

At the end of the day, after you have used your MasterTime form, reevaluate unfinished tasks. Do not worry about being unable to do everything you planned, since you did the most important things in priority under God's direction. Leave them to the Lord tonight and add them to tomorrow's list with the priority each deserves that day.

**Do not worry about being unable to do everything you planned, since you did the most important things in priority under God's direction.**

**Evaluate how often you feel that you accomplish the goals in "How to Use MasterTime." Circle the appropriate number: 4 = always, 3 = usually, 2 = often, 1 = sometimes. Then pray about areas in which you need to improve.**

I trust the Lord to direct me in all I do.
4    3    2    1
I plan my daily work under the Master's leadership.
4    3    2    1
I ask the Lord to bless my plans.
4    3    2    1
I depend on the Lord to direct my actions.
4    3    2    1

**Now begin to plan your time, using "How to Use MasterTime" and the MasterTime form on page 138. Use the MasterTime principles for at least the next six weeks. Feel free to make copies of the form as needed. If you already use another system for time management, apply these same principles to that process.**

Stop and pray, asking God to help you establish Christ-honoring priorities and to help you use your time wisely.

## LEARNING THE DISCIPLE'S CROSS

You can use the Disciple's Cross to keep your time priorities balanced and to work toward the goals in "How to Use MasterTime." The cross shows two means of intake for a Christian: prayer and God's Word. It shows two means of output: fellowship and witness. You will study about witness in week 5. If you manage your life so that you keep a proper balance between intake and output, spiritual and physical growth, mental and social stimulation, and time for your needs and those of others, you can keep ministering to others without depleting your spiritual resources.

**If you manage your life so that you keep a proper balance, you can keep ministering to others without depleting your spiritual resources.**

To summarize what you have learned this week, draw the portions of the Disciple's Cross you have studied, with the verses that accompany each discipline. At the next group session be ready to explain what you have learned about the cross.

## HAS THIS WEEK MADE A DIFFERENCE?

**Review "My Walk with the Master This Week" at the beginning of this week's material. Mark the activities you have finished by drawing vertical lines in the diamonds beside them. Finish any incomplete activities. Think about what you will say during your group session about your work on these activities.**

As you complete your study of "Fellowship with Believers," I hope that you asked Christ to examine areas in which you are not loving others as He commanded. Sometimes this kind of examination is uncomfortable. Your best intentions will not make you a disciple of Christ until you follow His command about fellowship and loving others.

# WEEK 5

# *Witness to the World*

## This Week's Goal

You will bear witness of Christ and your relationship with Him.

## My Walk with the Master This Week

You will complete the following activities to develop the six biblical disciplines. When you have completed each activity, draw a vertical line in the diamond beside it.

SPEND TIME WITH THE MASTER
◇ Have a daily quiet time. Check the box beside each day you have a quiet time this week: ❏ Sunday ❏ Monday ❏ Tuesday ❏ Wednesday ❏ Thursday ❏ Friday ❏ Saturday

LIVE IN THE WORD
◇ Read your Bible every day. Write what God says to you and what you say to God.
◇ Memorize John 15:8.
◇ Review Luke 9:23, John 15:5, John 8:31-32, John 15:7, and John 13:34-35.
◇ Study the reasons for memorizing Scripture in "How to Memorize Scripture."

PRAY IN FAITH
◇ Pray about your priorities and use of time.
◇ Pray for the members of your *MasterLife* group.

FELLOWSHIP WITH BELIEVERS
◇ Share with your prayer partner some of your problems and pray about your and your partner's needs.

WITNESS TO THE WORLD
◇ Review "How to Use MasterTime." Use it to plan your days and week.
◇ Make a new friend who is not a Christian. Learn all you can about your new friend and be ready to tell your *MasterLife* group about him or her.

MINISTER TO OTHERS
◇ Continue learning the Disciple's Cross. Explain the meaning of the left cross-bar to add to the information you have already learned.

## This Week's Scripture-Memory Verse

*" 'This is to my Father's glory, that you bear much fruit, showing yourselves to be my disciples' " (John 15:8).*

# DAY 1

## *Bearing Fruit for Christ*

**The Holy Spirit empowers us to witness.**

After I made my initial commitment as a college student to be Christ's disciple, I felt a strong need to begin to witness. About four nights a week I began going to a rescue mission operated by college students. I thought I would witness there, but no one came to Christ. I would memorize Scriptures to counter the excuses I would hear when people rejected the gospel. Armed with about 50 Scriptures, I could answer almost any objection, but I had not discovered the real secret: the Holy Spirit is the one who empowers us to witness. He bears witness through us. When I allowed Him to fill me, the persons to whom I witnessed began to trust Christ. Book 2 discusses being filled with the Spirit.

*" 'This is to my Father's glory, that you bear much fruit, showing yourselves to be my disciples' " (John 15:8).*

### A NATURAL DESIRE TO SHARE

Christ intends for His disciples to bear fruit. Your memory verse this week, John 15:8, says the way to show that you are His disciple is to bear much fruit. If you have an obedient relationship with Christ, you will want to share with friends about that relationship. Just as a woman who is getting married wants to talk about her fiancé, you will want to talk about Christ. The branch that lives in the Vine bears fruit. If you practice the disciplines around the Disciple's Cross, you have a desire to share with non-Christians. If you fellowship with God's people as you live daily in the Word and pray in faith, you naturally and normally share with others the Christ who lives in you. When God's love flows through the Son to you and others, you want to share the good news of Christ with those around you. The Holy Spirit will empower you to do so.

**When God's love flows through the Son to you and others, you want to share the good news of Christ with those around you.**

 **What does John 15:8 say you will do to show that you are Christ's disciple?**

_____

**How does John 15:8 say that you bring glory to God?**

_____

If you are Christ's disciple, you show it by bearing fruit for Him. You do this as a natural result of following Him. You do not do it in your own strength, as I tried to do at first. You allow the Holy Spirit to empower you for the task. When you bear fruit for Him, you bring glory to the Father. The Lord uses you to teach others about Himself.

## THE FRUIT OF A LIFE IN CHRIST

What exactly does Christ mean when He talks about bearing fruit? Galatians 5:22-23, in the margin, describes the fruit of the Spirit—the traits of Christ that the Holy Spirit produces when you abide in Christ. How does fruit bearing relate to your life in Christ?

 Read aloud John 15:8, this week's Scripture-memory verse, in the margin. What is the fruit you are expected to produce?
❏ The fruit of the Spirit, as listed in Galatians 5:22-23
❏ Producing other Christians

*"The fruit of the Spirit is love, joy, peace, patience, kindness, goodness, faithfulness, gentleness and self-control. Against such things there is no law"* (Gal. 5:22-23).

*" 'This is to my Father's glory, that you bear much fruit, showing yourselves to be my disciples' "* (John 15:8).

Actually, both answers are correct. To understand more clearly the purpose of fruit bearing, consider what occurs when a vine produces grapes. A vine does not produce fruit just so that a person can eat; it also enables the seed from that plant to be scattered. You are a Christian not merely to produce the sweet fruit of good deeds and good actions. As a Christian, you live a life that reflects those Christlike traits. The fruit of the Spirit mentioned in Galatians 5:22-23 naturally flows from your life if you abide in Christ. The result of your fruit bearing is to produce other Christians.

To illustrate, let's identify some of the things the world, with all its troubles and difficulties, needs.

**Check the qualities from Galatians 5:22-23 that the world needs.**
❏ love ❏ patience ❏ faithfulness
❏ joy ❏ kindness ❏ gentleness
❏ peace ❏ goodness ❏ self-control

Is love one of the things you checked that the world needs? Certainly, the world needs love, but most people look for it in the wrong places. One way you can exhibit Christ's character is to demonstrate love, for example, in loving your enemy. When others see you do that, they may be puzzled. They may ask: "How can you love like that? How can you love persons who mistreat you?" That is your opportunity for the seed to sprout. You can say, "The truth is, I can't love like that, but Christ can love that person through me." Your life is a witness, but a verbal witness is also necessary to glorify God instead of yourself. To accept credit for your good deeds would be wrong, because that is your chance to give credit to Christ. Only through Christ can you love your enemy. Demonstrating this fruit of the Spirit enables you to plant a seed that bears fruit.

**The result of your fruit bearing is to produce other Christians.**

**What would happen if you demonstrated love without telling others why?**

**A follower of Christ confesses Christ as the reason for his or her love.**

If you planted the seed without telling others why, they would think you are just different than they are. Along with demonstrating the fruit of the Spirit, a follower of Christ confesses Christ as the reason for his or her love. You have an opportunity to witness when you plant the seed of love and it bears fruit in your life. The Lord uses you to teach others about Himself.

You may have also answered that the world needs peace—which people also look for in the wrong places. When they see peace in your life that is different from the world's chaos, they wonder what makes you different. But if you do not tell them that you are peaceful and serene in the face of chaos because of Christ's peace that lives in you, they will not understand the source. If a person comments on your calmness when you confront difficulty, you can respond, "Can I tell you an experience I had with Christ that helps me respond this way?" This is a good way to introduce Christ as the source of your peace.

The world genuinely needs joy. You can be a joyful person and can radiate that joy. Instead of being disheartened when you encounter difficulties, you may look on the positive side. If people notice that you look for the good in a bad situation or that you refuse to give up when you are sick, they take notice. If you confess Christ as the source of joy in your life, you produce the fruit Christ desires for His disciples.

**We have looked at three fruit of the Spirit mentioned in Galatians 5:22-23—love, joy, and peace—and ways they could lead to a witness. Now choose one of the remaining fruit and describe how it could become the seed of a verbal witness.**
❑ patience      ❑ faithfulness
❑ kindness      ❑ gentleness
❑ goodness      ❑ self-control

_____

_____

THE FRUIT OF NEW BELIEVERS
As you have learned, bearing fruit can mean having the fruit of the Spirit in your life. Bearing fruit also includes the result: producing another follower of Christ. Jesus said in Matthew 4:19, " 'Follow me, and I will make you fishers of men.' " Fruit bearing is the normal, natural result of a life that has Christ at the center.

**Bearing fruit also includes producing another follower of Christ.**

You might wonder: *How do I learn to witness, since all of my friends are Christians? I'm willing to be obedient and bear fruit, but how can I find someone with whom I can share the gospel?* One way is to broaden your horizons, to reach beyond your comfortable circle of friends. You have persons all around you with whom you can become acquainted. Perhaps the following assignment will help.

Make a new friend this week who is not a Christian. Learn all you can about your new friend. Make notes and be ready to tell your *MasterLife* group about him or her.

_____

_____

## LEARNING THE DISCIPLE'S CROSS

This week introduces you to the fourth bar of the Disciple's Cross, witness to the world. Just as the vertical crossbar represents the two ways a disciple relates to God—through the Word and prayer—the horizontal crossbar represents the two ways a disciple relates to others—through fellowship and witness. The cross illustrates a disciple's balanced life in Christ.

Draw the portions of the Disciple's Cross you have already studied. Now draw the left crossbar and write the discipline witness on it. Refer to the completed cross on page 136 if you need help with your drawing.

In your quiet time today read Galatians 5, the chapter containing the verses you studied about the fruit of the Spirit. When you have read it, complete the Daily Master Communication Guide in the margin.

**DAILY MASTER COMMUNICATION GUIDE**

**GALATIANS 5**

**What God said to me:**

_____

_____

_____

_____

_____

_____

_____

**What I said to God:**

_____

_____

_____

_____

_____

_____

_____

# DAY 2

## *Relying on Christ*

**I kept Christ as my source of power instead of relying on my own strength, and the man was saved.**

As the Holy Spirit worked through me and as I began to witness more effectively, I often witnessed on the streets and in bars. One night when I witnessed in a bar, I talked with a man who seemed to be under deep conviction about his need for salvation. As we talked, he wept, but he would not receive Christ as Savior.

At that time the barkeeper told me that I was not welcome in his bar and made me leave. I was crushed, because the man with whom I had conversed was so burdened. When I left the bar, I went across the street to my car, knelt in the back seat, and pleaded with the Lord to lead the man to give his life to Christ. At that time I heard a tapping noise and looked up. Standing beside my car was the man to whom I had witnessed. We talked for a few minutes, and he trusted Christ. This was an answer to prayer, illustrating how God uses all six disciplines of the Disciple's Cross to accomplish His purposes. I kept Christ as my source of power instead of relying on my own strength, and the man was saved.

**Has Christ been your power source when you have witnessed? Describe an occasion when, as you witnessed, Christ was giving you the words to say and the strength to say them.**

_____

_____

*" 'I am the true vine, and my Father is the gardener. He cuts off every branch in me that bears no fruit, while every branch that does bear fruit he prunes so that it will be even more fruitful. You are already clean because of the word I have spoken to you. Remain in me, and I will remain in you' "* (John 15:1-4).

**Read John 15:1-4 in the margin. Then mark the statements that are true.**
❑ **Fruit bearing is not a choice for a Christian.**
❑ **Some Christians are expected to bear fruit, while others are not.**
❑ **Christ cleanses you so that you can bear more fruit.**
❑ **Fruit bearing depends on remaining in Christ.**

You may have the idea that witnessing is only for persons with outgoing personalities. You may think that you are excused from witnessing if you are not particularly talkative or do not have time. You may think that witnessing is not your major strength. But John 15:1-4 says that persons who are in Christ bear fruit. It does not say that only a few believers are fruit bearers. All Christians are expected to bear fruit. Christ made you clean through His Word so that you can bear more fruit. You cannot bear fruit apart from Him, as I learned during my futile attempts to witness in my own strength. When Christ became my source and I shared from my lifelong, obedient relationship with Him,

I became more effective in witnessing. In the previous exercise all of the statements are true except the second one.

**Have you ever made excuses for not witnessing?** ❑ **Yes** ❑ **No**

 Try to say John 15:8, this week's Scripture-memory verse, several times from memory. Write what it says about making excuses for not witnessing.

_____

_____

You may have answered something like this: The verse indicates that Christ's disciples bear fruit. If I want to be His disciple, no excuse is really valid for not witnessing.

How are you doing with the discipline of memorizing Scripture? By now you have likely memorized several verses you can use in various situations. I have found Scripture memorization helpful in times of temptation, trial, and testimony. When I am tempted, I remember 1 Corinthians 10:13, one of the earliest Scriptures I memorized. The Holy Spirit uses that verse to assure me that He will not allow me to be tempted more than I can bear but will offer an escape every time. Many times I have faced trials I could not understand. Each time the Holy Spirit reminded me of James 1:2-3: "Consider it pure joy, my brothers, whenever you face trials of many kinds, because you know that the testing of your faith develops perseverance. Perseverance must finish its work so that you may be mature and complete, not lacking anything."

**By now, the fifth week of your study, you have likely memorized five verses and are beginning to learn a sixth. Describe situations when having memorized these verses helped you. Be ready to share what you have written at your next group session.**

Luke 9:23: _____

John 15:5: _____

John 8:31-32: _____

John 15:7: _____

John 13:34-35: _____

 Read Acts 8:26-40, about Philip's witness to the Ethiopian, during your quiet time today. Then complete the Daily Master Communication Guide in the margin.

## DAILY MASTER COMMUNICATION GUIDE

ACTS 8:26-40

**What God said to me:**

_____

_____

_____

_____

_____

_____

_____

**What I said to God:**

_____

_____

_____

_____

_____

_____

_____

_____

_____

# DAY 3

*Every Disciple's Orders*

**Witnessing is part of every disciple's marching orders.**

*" 'You did not choose me, but I chose you and appointed you to go and bear fruit—fruit that will last. Then the Father will give you whatever you ask in my name' " (John 15:16).*

**M**aybe you think that witnessing is something Jesus expects only of preachers, evangelists, or missionaries. You may think that Jesus does not expect ordinary Christians to bear fruit for Him in this way. But John 15, the passage you have been reading, makes clear that witnessing is part of every disciple's marching orders.

**Read John 15:16 in the margin and answer the questions below.**

**What did Jesus say His purpose was in choosing the disciples?**

_____

**What did Jesus promise fruitful disciples they could do?**

_____

Fruit bearing was not optional for the disciples. It was expected of them as part of their lifelong, obedient relationships with Him. Jesus told the disciples that to bear fruit that would last was the reason He chose them. Along with this expectation Jesus gave a promise: that the disciples could pray in Christ's name and have their prayers answered. Obedient disciples seek to live in keeping with the Father's will and to pray accordingly.

WITNESSING IS NOT OPTIONAL
In John 15:27 Jesus once again told the disciples that witnessing is not optional; it is a discipline He expects. The verse says, " 'You also must testify, for you have been with me from the beginning.' "

**Why did Jesus tell the disciples that they must testify?**

_____

Jesus commanded the disciples to testify about Him because they had been with Him from the beginning and knew firsthand of His saving truth.

Again read John 15 in your quiet time today. Let God speak to you about the importance of bearing fruit and of testifying about Christ. After you have read this passage, complete the Daily Master Communication Guide on page 100.

Although you did not physically live alongside Jesus, as the disciples did, you know firsthand of His saving truth, and you experience a growing relationship with Him. You can tell others what Christ has done in your life just as the disciples did. You can tell others about Him, based on your experience.

As you study about witnessing to others, you may find yourself thinking: *I want to do that! I know that Christ wants me to be His witness. But how will I know the words to say? How do I know I won't freeze up or embarrass myself?*

**Read John 15:4 in the margin and complete this sentence:**

**I am unable to bear fruit unless I** _____.

*" 'Remain in me, and I will remain in you. No branch can bear fruit by itself; it must remain in the vine. Neither can you bear fruit unless you remain in me' " (John 15:4).*

No branch can bear fruit by itself. The branch is part of the vine; it is not just attached to the vine. As the the sap and the life-giving power that produces the fruit flow through the branch, they originate in the vine. The end of the branch that bears the fruit is the part you see, but the vine is always the life-giving source.

THE PROMISE OF CHRIST'S POWER
When you were saved, you became part of the Vine. You cannot bear fruit if you do not remain in the Vine, that is, stay in fellowship with Christ. If you stay in fellowship with Christ, you will be empowered to witness. In my early attempts at witnessing I learned that I could not succeed just because I willed myself to succeed. Only when I allowed the Holy Spirit to take control of my thoughts, my words, and my actions could I witness effectively.

**If you stay in fellowship with Christ, you will be empowered to witness.**

 **See if you can recall John 15:5, one of your previous Scripture-memory verses. What does it promise will happen if you remain in Christ?**

_____

The verse does not say that perhaps you will bear fruit or that only exceptional disciples will bear fruit. It says that if you remain in Christ, you will bear fruit. This is a precious promise from God's Word to you about what happens to a person who abides in Christ and witnesses to others. He will enable you to bear fruit if you remain in Him and seek His will.

**What are some ways you can remain in Christ so that you can bear fruit for Him?**
❏ **Live in the Word by studying it and memorizing it.**
❏ **Pray that the Father will direct you to witness according to His will.**

## DAILY MASTER COMMUNICATION GUIDE

### JOHN 15

**What God said to me:**

_____

_____

_____

_____

_____

_____

**What I said to God:**

_____

_____

_____

_____

_____

_____

❏ Fellowship with other believers to hear instruction from God's Word and to draw encouragement from the body of Christ.
❏ Have a daily quiet time to hear God speak to you.

**Which discipline do you most need to work on? Draw a star beside it. Then ask God to help you be more diligent in that practice.**

As you reviewed the above suggestions, how did you evaluate yourself on your practice of having a personal quiet time with God every day? I have found that nothing takes the place of a personal quiet time with God every day. Like manna, it does not last long enough to provide for tomorrow. If I write in my Daily Master Communication Guide each day, God says more and more to me. Then when times are difficult, I can go back and read what God said to me in the previous days, weeks, or months. Many times this perspective gives me new insights about my relationship with God and restores my spirit.

**Complete this statement: The time that works best for my daily quiet time is _____.**

If finding time for your daily, personal time with Christ is still a challenge for you, review what you learned in week 4 about ways to set priorities using MasterTime. Use MasterTime to plan your days and weeks.

Stop and pray, asking God to help you with your priorities and your use of time so that you will be able to find a consistent time every day to remain connected to the Vine.

You can also abide in Christ by fellowshipping with other believers and by expressing your care and concern for them. For example, the time you spend with your prayer partner can be a time of fellowship.

Share with your prayer partner some of your problems. Pray about your and your partner's needs. Before you finish your conversation, say John 15:8, this week's Scripture-memory verse, to your prayer partner.

As you studied in week 4, your fellowship with others naturally leads you to share Christ with them. The Lord will use you to teach others about Him. You will have fellowship as you demonstrate your love for fellow believers, as you did with your prayer partner. You also need to relate to persons who do not know Christ, attempting to bring them to a saving knowledge of Him. Continue to cultivate the friendship with your new non-Christian friend.

LEARNING THE DISCIPLE'S CROSS

To reinforce what you are learning, draw the portions of the Disciple's Cross you have studied. Now draw the left crossbar and write *witness* on it. Write *John 15:8,* the Scripture reference that accompanies the left crossbar, under *witness.*

# DAY 4

## *Compelled to Tell*

When I was six years old, I made my profession of faith in Christ while my father was attending Southwestern Baptist Theological Seminary in Fort Worth. As he was preaching a revival service in a local rescue mission, I recognized that I was a sinner and that if a trap door were under me, I would go straight to hell. Realizing that I needed to repent of my sins, I almost ran down the aisle. I felt that a burden had been lifted from me. With the enthusiasm of a new convert I told my neighbor, my barber, and even the president of the seminary that I had trusted Christ. I could not help telling what I had seen and heard.

**I could not help telling what I had seen and heard.**

WHAT HAS CHRIST DONE FOR YOU?

The Bible says, " 'We cannot help speaking about what we have seen and heard' " (Acts 4:20). Has Christ ever been so real to you that you could not help testifying about what you saw and heard? Perhaps He answered a prayer in such a direct, specific, or meaningful way that you responded, "Only the Lord could have done that!" Perhaps you experienced physical or emotional healing. Perhaps He provided you special encouragement or counsel from a friend just when you needed it. You did not live at the time of Christ to observe His miracles firsthand, but perhaps you have experienced modern-day miracles. If so, how can you refrain from telling persons you encounter how awesome Christ is?

**How ready are you to testify about what Christ has done in your life? Evaluate yourself by circling the appropriate number: 1 = sometimes, 2 = often, 3 = usually, 4 = always. Then pray about areas in which you need to improve.**

**I build relationships with non-Christian friends or acquaintances so that I can eventually have opportunities to witness to them.**
1    2    3    4

**I pray with persons or offer to pray for persons who have needs, and I remind them that God cares about them.    1    2    3    4**

**I visit or contact persons who visit my church and express concern for them.    1    2    3    4**

**I tell lost persons about Christ even though it means risking that they will reject me.    1    2    3    4**

**I do not hesitate to tell others when God answers my prayers.**
1    2    3    4

Do not feel embarrassed or awkward if you answered with a 1 on several or most of the statements in the exercise. Learning to share your faith boldly can be a building process. Book 2 provides techniques and skills for sharing your personal testimony.

MAKE SURE OF YOUR RELATIONSHIP

As you think about witnessing to the world, first be sure of your own salvation so that you can bear fruit. Be sure that you are connected to the Vine so that you have Christ's love flowing through you in a life-long, obedient relationship with Him. The following gospel presentation is called the Roman Road.[1] You will read eight passages from the Book of Romans that clearly explain the gospel message. Study the presentation to determine how you measure up in your relationship with Christ. You may want to memorize the verses or to mark them in sequence in your Bible so that you can also share the good news with others. *MasterLife 4: The Disciple's Mission* teaches you another gospel presentation you can use to witness.

**THE ROMAN ROAD**
1. **God's power can make you secure.**
2. **God's power results in change.**
3. **Sin makes change necessary.**
4. **God still loves you.**
5. **Sin earns death, but God offers life.**
6. **Confessing Jesus as Lord means that you recognize His rightful authority over you.**
7. **Repentance means changing the direction of your life and living a God-oriented life.**
8. **Believing means trusting Jesus with your life.**
9. **Calling on the name of the Lord means asking Him for forgiveness of sin and for salvation.**
10. **You now have hope.**
11. **Faith = life for God.**

## THE ROMAN ROAD

1. *God's power can make you secure.* Read Romans 1:16 in the margin. Many people today live without hope. They have no resources to strengthen them and guide them through their struggles in life. According to Romans 1:16, the focus of the Christian faith is the gospel, which is the good news that God's power is available to help you in whatever problems you face. Through Jesus Christ a power great enough to bring salvation and deliverance is available to any person who believes.

*"I am not ashamed of the gospel, because it is the power of God for the salvation of everyone who believes: first for the Jew, then for the Gentile"* (Rom. 1:16).

God's _____ can make you secure.

2. *God's power results in change.* Read Romans 2:4 in the margin. Through God's power, people can change. The biblical word for *change* is *repentance*. This means allowing God to change the direction of your life.

*"God's kindness leads you toward repentance"* (Rom. 2:4).

God's power results in _____.

3. *Sin makes change necessary.* Read Romans 3:23 in the margin. Why do people need to change? From what does Jesus offer deliverance? According to the Bible, every man and woman has a problem. The problem can be described in many ways, but the most common biblical word is *sin*. One meaning of *sin* is *to fall short of the mark God has set*. The Bible teaches that God's standard for us is Jesus Christ. If Jesus were standing in front of you in the flesh, could you say that you are as good as He is? The failure to meet God's standard is sin, which means that all people have a sin problem. You may do much that is good, and you may not want to do anything bad, but none of us can measure up to God's standard of always doing right.

*"All have sinned and fall short of the glory of God"* (Rom. 3:23).

_____ makes change necessary.

4. *God still loves you.* Read Romans 5:8 in the margin. Some people think that their failure to meet God's standard means that God is their enemy. Because they do not live up to His expectations, God must be against them. But the message of Jesus is that in spite of our sin, God still loves us.

God's love for you is not based on ignorance and an unawareness of sin. Nor is it based on a tolerance that overlooks your sin. Knowing your sin, God chose to love you, even though it meant His Son's death for you. In doing what was necessary to overcome your problem with sin, God demonstrated the depth and reality of His love for you (also see John 3:16).

*"God demonstrates his own love for us in this: While we were still sinners, Christ died for us"* (Rom. 5:8).

God still _____ you.

*"The wages of sin is death, but the gift of God is eternal life in Christ Jesus our Lord" (Rom. 6:23).*

5. *Sin earns death, but God offers life.* Read Romans 6:23 in the margin. According to the Bible, the consequences of sin are too serious to overlook. Although God is not your enemy, He is your judge. As judge He cannot ignore your failure to meet His standard of perfection. Romans 6:23 says that "the wages of sin is death." Whenever you sin, you earn the wages of death. Since every person is guilty of sin, every person is subject to the consequences of eternal death and separation from God (see John 3:36; Rev. 20:11-15).

An alternative exists. Through your works you earn death, but "the gift of God is eternal life in Christ Jesus our Lord" (Rom. 6:23). Jesus died on the cross in your place (see 1 Pet. 3:18). He took your guilt for sin upon Himself so that His death would fulfill the judgment of God against your sin (see 2 Cor. 5:21; Col. 2:13-14). Your sin is judged in the death of Jesus on the cross as our substitute. By your works you earn death, but by His grace you can receive eternal life. God offers eternal life and the forgiveness of sin through Jesus Christ as His gift.

**Sin earns _____, but God offers _____.**

6. *Confessing Jesus as Lord means that you recognize His rightful authority over you.*

**Underline the words in Romans 10:9-10,13, in the margin, that indicate what you need to do to accept Christ as Savior and Lord.**

Read Romans 10:9-10,13 in the margin. The words *confess, believe,* and *call* summarize what someone must do to receive God's free gift and be saved.

The biblical word translated *confess* means *to say the same thing. Lord* may be translated *ruler, boss,* or *sovereign authority.* When we confess Jesus as Lord, we are saying the same thing about God that He says about Himself (see Isa. 45:5-7,22-24; Phil. 2:10-11). We recognize His rightful authority over us. In acknowledging Jesus as Lord, we admit our sin in failing to meet His standard of perfect obedience and righteousness.

**Confessing Jesus as Lord means that you recognize His**

**rightful _____ over you.**

*"If you confess with your mouth, 'Jesus is Lord,' and believe in your heart that God raised him from the dead, you will be saved. For it is with your heart that you believe and are justified, and it is with your mouth that you confess and are saved. For, 'Everyone who calls on the name of the Lord will be saved' " (Rom. 10:9-10,13).*

7. *Repentance means changing the direction of your life and living a God-oriented life.* To confess Jesus as Lord also means to repent of your sins. In accepting His rightful authority over you, you turn away from life on your terms in order to obey and serve

Him. This turning away from sin in order to follow Jesus is called repentance. More than feeling sorry, it is changing the direction of your life and living a God-oriented rather than a self-oriented life (see Luke 3:7-14).

**Repentance means changing the _____ of your**

**life and living a _____ life.**

8. *Believing means trusting Jesus with your life. Believe means to trust.* When you "believe in your heart that God raised him from the dead" (Rom. 10:9), you have confidence that the death and resurrection of Jesus are enough to secure your salvation. You trust in the work of Christ rather than in the work of your life for your salvation. When you look at a bridge, you might know that it would hold you up if you crossed it. The bridge never actually holds you up, however, until you get on it and cross. Similarly, you may know a lot about Jesus, but until you trust Him with your life, putting your life into His hands, you are not believing in Him. To believe in Jesus is to put your life, both physically and spiritually, into His hands.

**Believing means _____ Jesus with your life.**

When you acknowledge that Jesus is the rightful Lord or boss of your life and when you are willing to believe in Him, trusting in His work alone for your salvation, you need only call on Him to be saved. In Romans 10:13 Paul wrote, " 'Everyone who calls on the name of the Lord will be saved.' " Note how broad the invitation is. *Anyone* who is willing to call on the name of the Lord will be saved. No other qualifications are needed. If you are willing to call on Him, you can be saved.

*Anyone* **who is willing to call on the name of the Lord will be saved.**

9. *Calling on the name of the Lord means asking Him for forgiveness of sin and for salvation.* When you ask Him for salvation, you are acknowledging Him as your Lord and expressing your intention to live a life of obedience and service. Persons who call on Him will be saved.

**Calling on the name of the Lord means asking Him for**

**_____ of sin and for _____ .**

**The three words that summarize what someone must do to be**

**saved are: _____ , _____ , _____ .**

"The Spirit himself testifies with our spirit that we are God's children. Now if we are children, then we are heirs—heirs of God and co-heirs with Christ, if indeed we share in his sufferings in order that we may also share in his glory. For I am convinced that neither death nor life, neither angels nor demons, neither the present nor the future, nor any powers, neither height nor depth, nor anything else in all creation, will be able to separate us from the love of God that is in Christ Jesus our Lord" (Rom. 8:16-17,38-39).

"I urge you, brothers, in view of God's mercy, to offer your bodies as living sacrifices, holy and pleasing to God—this is your spiritual act of worship. Do not conform any longer to the pattern of this world, but be transformed by the renewing of your mind. Then you will be able to test and approve what God's will is—his good, pleasing and perfect will" (Rom. 12:1-2).

As you have proceeded through *MasterLife 1: The Disciple's Cross*, you may have experienced some questions about where you stand in your commitment to Christ. As you have read about being totally committed to Christ, you may not be able to state firmly that you have taken that initial step of following Him that occurs when you receive Christ in salvation. *Master-Life* was designed for persons who have accepted Jesus as their Savior and Lord and who want to learn what it means to be His true followers. If you find that you cannot say with 100-percent surety that you have made that commitment, you can accept Him now by inviting Him into your life. If you wish, use this sample prayer to express your commitment:

*Lord Jesus, I need You. I want You to be my Savior and my Lord. I accept Your death on the cross as the payment for my sins, and I now entrust my life to Your care. Thank You for forgiving me and for giving me new life. Please help me grow as a Christian so that my life will bring glory and honor to You. Amen.*

_____     _____
Signed                                                         Date

Receiving Christ does not guarantee that you will not struggle with issues like self-denial, cross bearing, and following Jesus. It does not mean that you will not be tempted to give your devotion to someone or something else. It does not mean that you will not shy away from the costs of discipleship. It means that He forgives you; that He has a lasting relationship with you that extends into eternity; and that He will grant you strength, power, and wisdom as you seek to be His disciple. I suggest that you talk with your *MasterLife* leader, your pastor, a church-staff member, or a trusted Christian friend about any new commitment you have made.

10. *You now have hope.* Read Romans 8:16-17,38-39 in the margin. When you are saved, God adopts you as His child, and His Holy Spirit assures you that you are part of His family. According to Roman law at the time of Paul's writing, someone's adopted son also became his heir. While Christ is God's heir by nature, Christians have become God's heirs by adoption. Therefore, you are a joint-heir with Christ.

Verses 38-39 say that you are eternally secure in God. Because Christ has defeated the principalities and powers of this earth, you need not fear human and superhuman enemies. Nothing can separate you from God's love in Christ Jesus.

As a believer, you can live with hope because you are a child of God and are secure in His love.

**You now have** _____.

11. *Faith = life for God.* Read Romans 12:1-2 in the margin on the previous page. When you become a Christian, you begin to live your life for God. You can expect your life to be different. God wants your life to change as you follow Jesus, even if it means sacrifice. The goal for believers is to look and live less like the unsaved people of the world and more like Jesus. That kind of change happens because God brings it about. He will transform your life, making it more like the life of Jesus (see Phil. 1:6; 2:13). Jesus will make you look and live like one of His children as you follow Him.

**Faith = life for** _____.

## YOU ARE HIS WITNESS

Whether you just received Christ or have been His disciple for many years, you are His witness. You may want to learn the previous presentation so that you can explain to a lost person how to receive eternal life. You may first want to accompany your *MasterLife* leader when he or she uses it to witness to an unsaved person.

Do not be afraid to share your salvation experience with non-Christians. In *MasterLife 2: The Disciple's Personality* you will learn how to share your personal salvation experience. In *MasterLife 3: The Disciple's Victory* you will learn how to use a booklet to share the way someone can become a Christian. In *MasterLife 4: The Disciple's Mission* you will learn how to use another presentation to lead lost persons to receive Christ as Savior and Lord.

**Read Acts 16:11-15, describing Paul's witness to Lydia, during your quiet time today. Then complete the Daily Master Communication Guide in the margin.**

**Pray for each of your *MasterLife* group members by name. Ask God to help each person receive a blessing from *MasterLife* and especially from the gospel presentation you have studied. Ask Him to help you be available as a friend to your fellow members.**

**Continue to memorize John 15:8, this week's Scripture-memory verse, which goes with the left crossbar of the Disciple's Cross. On a sheet of paper, write the verse from one to three times.**

---

**DAILY MASTER COMMUNICATION GUIDE**

ACTS 16:11-15

**What God said to me:**

_____

_____

_____

_____

_____

_____

_____

_____

**What I said to God:**

_____

_____

_____

_____

_____

_____

_____

_____

> *" 'Remember the words I spoke to you: "No servant is greater than his master." If they persecuted me, they will persecute you also. If they obeyed my teaching, they will obey yours also. They will treat you this way because of my name, for they do not know the One who sent me' " (John 15:20-21).*

> *"While he was still speaking a crowd came up, and the man who was called Judas, one of the Twelve, was leading them. He approached Jesus to kiss him, but Jesus asked him, 'Judas, are you betraying the Son of Man with a kiss?' " (Luke 22:47-48).*

> *"Jesus left there and went to his hometown, accompanied by his disciples. When the Sabbath came, he began to teach in the synagogue, and many who heard him were amazed. 'Where did this man get these things?' they asked. 'What's this wisdom that has been given him, that he even does miracles! Isn't this the carpenter? Isn't this Mary's son and the brother of James, Joseph, Judas and Simon? Aren't his sisters here with us?' And they took offense at him" (Mark 6:1-3).*

> *"He then began to teach them that the Son of Man must suffer many things and be rejected by the elders, chief priests and teachers of the law, and that he must be killed and after three days must rise again" (Mark 8:31).*

## DAY 5

# The Price of Bearing Fruit

**H**igh-school principal John Eluru was rehearsing to play the role of Jesus in the Ugandan translation of the *Jesus* film, a riveting movie about the life of Christ. The film has brought countless people to Christ in every corner of the globe. As crews carried John and other film personnel from their Ugandan village to the production site, guerrilla fighters burst onto the road and fired. John was shot in the heart.

That night as John lay dying, he urged the film technician: "Don't stop the dubbing. Uganda needs this film. I have done my part, but don't stop the work, and don't ever be afraid." The next morning John died, but today every time the completed film is shown in Uganda, John's voice as Jesus tells hundreds of people how to know Christ.[2]

Being Christ's disciple does not occur without sacrifice. Witnessing to the world as you bear fruit for Christ has its price. As John 15:20-21, in the margin, reveals, when you have a relationship with Him, you will be persecuted, just as He suffered. Everything you endure for Christ, He endured also. He knew rejection and suffering, and so will you.

**In John 15:20-21 what do Jesus' words "No servant is greater than his master" mean to you?**

_____

_____

YOUR COMPANION IN SUFFERING
You are subject to the same rejection Jesus encountered. The same type of hard-hearted, closed-minded people who rejected the Master will also reject you. In contrast, the same type of people who were open to His teachings while He was on earth will be open to your words and deeds today.

**What did Christ suffer for you? Read the three verses in the margin. Then match the statements in the right column with the correct references on the left.**

___ 1. Luke 22:47-48    **a. Respected persons in authority rejected Him.**
___ 2. Mark 6:1-3
___ 3. Mark 8:31      **b. A friend betrayed Him.**

                        **c. The people in His hometown took offense at Him.**

**Go back and draw a star beside any type of persecution you have experienced.**

Have you had an experience in which you felt persecuted because you witnessed for Christ? ❑ Yes ❑ No If so, describe it below.

_____

_____

How does it make you feel to realize that Christ has already endured any type of heartache you have suffered?

_____

Christ's suffering for you was so great that listing all of the trials He endured on earth would be impossible in this book. The Scriptures in the margin on page 108 represent only a few. Likewise, because of Christ-honoring stands you take, you sometimes experience the rejection of friends, family, neighbors, your community, and people you respect. I hope as you thought about the fact that Christ is your companion in suffering, you described feeling strengthened and encouraged by considering the depths of His love for you. The correct answers to the previous matching exercise are 1. b, 2. c, 3.a.

**Because of Christ-honoring stands you take, you sometimes experience the rejection.**

LEARNING THE DISCIPLE'S CROSS
After studying the Disciple's Cross for five weeks, you know that the left crossbar represents bearing fruit by witnessing. The Disciple's Cross itself embodies fruit bearing. If you learn and practice the six disciplines, you will live an obedient life and thus will bear fruit.

 Again draw the Disciple's Cross, writing *witness* on the left crossbar. Also include *John 15:8*, the Scripture that accompanies the left crossbar.

## DAILY MASTER COMMUNICATION GUIDE

MATTHEW 4:1-11

**What God said to me:**

_____

_____

_____

_____

_____

_____

**What I said to God:**

_____

_____

_____

_____

_____

_____

_____

_____

To reinforce what you are learning about fruit bearing as a characteristic of a disciple, say aloud John 15:8, this week's Scripture-memory verse. Recite it to a family member or to someone you regularly see in the course of your day.

SCRIPTURE MEMORIZATION: A KEY TO BEARING FRUIT
Each day you have been asked to memorize Scripture. I hope you will not look at this merely as busy work or as course requirements. Memorizing Scripture enables you to claim victory over Satan, to claim victory over sin, to win others to Christ, to meditate on the Word, and to direct your daily life. Most important of all, you memorize Scripture because God commands it.

Try to memorize in your own words the six reasons listed in the following chart.

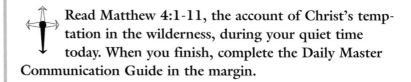

**REASONS TO MEMORIZE SCRIPTURE**
1. To claim victory over Satan.

Read Matthew 4:1-11, the account of Christ's temptation in the wilderness, during your quiet time today. When you finish, complete the Daily Master Communication Guide in the margin.

a. Jesus set the example. Read Matthew 4:7,10.
b. Satan sometimes misuses the Scriptures. Compare Matthew 4:6 with Psalm 91:11-12:

_He will command his angels concerning you_
_to guard you in all your ways;_
_they will lift you up in their hands,_
_so that you will not strike your foot against a stone._

c. The Word is the sword of the Spirit:

_How can a young man keep his way pure?_
_By living according to your word._
_I have hidden your word in my heart_
_that I might not sin against you (Ps. 119:9,11)._

2. **To claim victory over sin.** See Psalm 119:9,11.
3. **To win others to Christ.**
a. You will always be ready to give an answer about your faith: "Always be prepared to give an answer to everyone who asks you to give the reason for the hope that you have" (1 Pet. 3:15).

b. The Holy Spirit can bring to mind the word that is needed for any situation: " 'When he, the Spirit of truth, comes, he will guide you into all truth. He will not speak on his own; he will speak only what he hears, and he will tell you what is yet to come' " (John 16:13).

c. Understanding the Word will make you bold in your witness: "After they prayed, the place where they were meeting was shaken. And they were all filled with the Holy Spirit and spoke the word of God boldly" (Acts 4:31).

**Understanding the Word will make you bold in your witness.**

**4. To meditate on the Word.**

> *His delight is in the law of the Lord,*
> *and on his law he meditates day and night.*
> *He is like a tree planted by streams of water,*
> *which yields its fruit in season*
> *and whose leaf does not wither (Ps. 1:2-3).*

**5. To direct your daily life.**

> *Your word is a lamp to my feet*
> *and a light for my path (Ps. 119:105).*

**6. Because God commands it.** " 'These commandments that I give you today are to be upon your hearts' " (Deut. 6:6). "Let the word of Christ dwell in you richly as you teach and admonish one another with all wisdom, and as you sing psalms, hymns, and spiritual songs with gratitude in your hearts to God" (Col. 3:16).

**Memorize Scripture because God commands it.**

**Give an example of how memorizing Scripture has helped you in one of the above ways.**

_____

_____

_____

Read on the following page the suggestions for memorizing Scripture. Check any suggestion you have tried. Draw a star beside any you pledge to try.

**Review is the most important secret of Scripture memorization.**

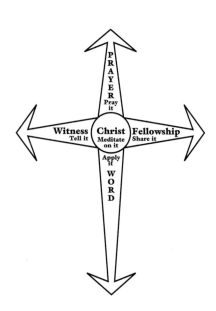

## HOW TO MEMORIZE SCRIPTURE

1. Choose a verse that speaks to your need or, if the verse is assigned, discover how it meets a particular need in your life.

2. Understand the verse. Read the verse in relation to its context. Read the verse in various translations.

3. Record memory verses on a cassette tape so that you can listen to them. Leave a space after each verse so that you can practice quoting it. Then record the verse a second time so that you can hear it again after you have quoted it.

4. Locate and underline the verse in your Bible so that you can see where it is on the page.

5. Write the verse on a card, including the Scripture reference and the topic it addresses. This allows you to relate the verse to a particular subject so that you can find it when a need arises.

6. Place the written verse in prominent places so that you can review it while you do other tasks. Put it over the kitchen sink, on the bathroom mirror, on the dashboard for reviewing at stop lights, and on the refrigerator.

7. Commit the verse to memory. Divide it into natural, meaningful phrases and learn it word by word. If you learn it word-perfect in the beginning, it will be set in your memory, will be easier to review, will give you boldness when you are tempted, and will convince the person with whom you are sharing that he or she can trust your word.

8. Review, review, review. This is the most important secret of Scripture memorization. Review a new verse at least once a day for six weeks. Review the verse weekly for the next six weeks and then monthly for the rest of your life.

9. Use these activities to set a verse in your mind: see it in pictorial form; sing it, making up your own tune; pray it back to God; do it by making it a part of your life; and use it as often as possible.

10. Use the version of the Disciple's Cross in the margin to master the verse. Note that you can make the Scriptures a part of every facet of your life (see John 8:31-32).

11. Have someone check your memorization. Or write the verse from memory and then check it yourself, using your Bible.

12. Make Scripture memorization fun. Make a game of remembering verses with your family and friends. A game I have used is to cite a reference to a *MasterLife* group member before the person can cite it to me. For instance, if you cite John 15:5, the other person must quote it. If the other person says the reference first, you must quote it.

13. Set a goal for the number of verses you will memorize each week. State your goal: _____ per week. Do not try to learn too many verses so fast that you do not have time for daily review, which is essential to memorizing Scripture.

Since review helps you memorize, go back and work on this week's Scripture-memory verse. Choose one of the suggestions you read and practice it to reinforce your memorization of John 15:8.

If you have not already done so, write the verses you are memorizing in *MasterLife 1: The Disciple's Cross* on cards that you can carry with you. Review them often.

## HAS THIS WEEK MADE A DIFFERENCE?

**Review "My Walk with the Master This Week" at the beginning of this week's material. Mark the activities you have finished by drawing vertical lines in the diamonds beside them. Finish any incomplete activities. Think about what you will say during your group session about your work on these activities.**

Think about your study of "Witness to the World" this week.
- Have you resolved to work on developing new relationships with persons who do not know Christ?
- Have your relationships with non-Christian friends taken on new meaning because of this week's study?
- Have you identified opportunities to witness that you had not thought about previously?
- Have you committed to bear fruit in a new way?

I hope that this week's study has prompted you to make new commitments in your continuing effort to abide in Christ and to develop your lifelong, obedient relationship with Him. Making new commitments requires honesty, because you may realize that you need to make improvements in your life. Look on these as opportunities to grow rather than judging your old ways of doing things.

**Making new commitments requires honesty, because you may realize that you need to make improvements in your life.**

---

[1]Adapted from Chuck Kelley, *Learning to Share My Faith* (Nashville: LifeWay Press, 1994), 27–34.
[2]Paul Eshleman, *The Touch of Jesus* (Orlando: NewLife, 1995), 157–58.

## WEEK 6

# Minister to Others

## This Week's Goal

You will minister to others as you take up your cross and follow Jesus.

## My Walk with the Master This Week

You will complete the following activities to develop the six biblical disciplines. When you have completed each activity, draw a vertical line in the diamond beside it.

 SPEND TIME WITH THE MASTER
◇ Have a daily quiet time. Check the box beside each day you have a quiet time this week: ❑ Sunday ❑ Monday ❑ Tuesday
❑ Wednesday ❑ Thursday ❑ Friday ❑ Saturday

 LIVE IN THE WORD
◇ Read your Bible every day. Write what God says to you and what you say to God.
◇ Memorize John 15:13.
◇ Review Luke 9:23, John 15:5, John 8:31-32, John 15:7, John 13:34-35, and John 15:8.

 PRAY IN FAITH
◇ Pray for your pastor and your church.
◇ Pray for the lost persons the group members talked about at the previous session.
◇ Ask God to lead you as you plan your time with Him, using the MasterTime form.

 FELLOWSHIP WITH BELIEVERS
◇ Share with someone what the Lord has done for you since you have been involved in *MasterLife*.

 WITNESS TO THE WORLD
◇ Use MasterTime to plan your days.
◇ Do a kind act for your new non-Christian friend this week. Learn all you can about your new friend. Be ready to tell your *MasterLife* group what happened.

 MINISTER TO OTHERS
◇ Finish learning the Disciple's Cross. Be ready to share it with a member of your *MasterLife* group before the Growing Disciples Workshop. Say all of the verses that go with the Disciple's Cross.

## This Week's Scripture-Memory Verse

" 'Greater love has no one than this, that he lay down his life for his friends' "
(John 15:13).

## DAY 1

~

# Take Up Your Cross

A group of people rushed into the room where my friend, a Christian relief worker in central Asia, was ministering. They pleaded, "Please come help this old man, or he will die!" In the war-torn area of the country where my friend served, mine fields were plentiful. The concerned individuals who pressed him to help had found a shepherd injured by a mine. My friend knew that he must quickly decide what to do. "I knew it was not wise to enter a mine field, but I felt that the Lord wanted me to help this person in need," my friend recalled. "As I crossed the field, I noticed that everyone following me was walking single file in my footsteps."

My friend at last located the man, carried him to the road, and hailed a truck. He begged the truck driver to carry the injured shepherd to a hospital, but no occupant of the crowded vehicle would give up his place. To a worker who spoke English my friend said, "Tell the truck driver that I will pay twice what any rider paid if you will take this man to the hospital." The worker, in translating to the truck driver, commented, "This Christian is going to pay the man's way when we Muslims won't do anything." At that point the truck driver refused the money and made a place for the injured man.

In this central-Asian country where Christianity is not accepted, this modern-day Good Samaritan story spread all over the countryside with the message "This is what a Christian does. This is the kind of service a Christian does in Jesus' name."

## WHAT A CHRISTIAN DOES

When Christ is at the center of your life, how do you serve others? What does being a disciple of Christ lead you to do? Although you may not serve as a relief worker in a war-torn country as my friend does, your opportunities for sacrificial service for others are endless.

**Your opportunities for sacrificial service for others are endless.**

**Describe an occasion when you served someone sacrificially.**

_____

_____

**What opportunities for service do you have that you are not taking advantage of?**

_____

**Every Christian is a minister if he or she follows Jesus and serves others as He did.**

You probably identified someone in need or opportunities for sacrificial service in Jesus' name. The type of ministry we are examining does not mean being a pastor or another church minister. Every Christian is a minister if he or she follows Jesus and serves others as He did.

BEARING YOUR CROSS
To learn how a disciple ministers to others, start by reviewing one of your first memory verses, Luke 9:23, in which Jesus outlined the three basic commitments of a disciple.

 **Complete Luke 9:23 below by filling in the blanks. Then say this verse from memory.**

" 'If anyone would come after me, he must _____ himself and take up his _____ daily and _____ me.' "

The three basic commitments a disciple makes are to deny self, take up his or her cross, and follow Christ. In week 1 when you learned about putting Christ at the center of your life, you focused on self-denial. In week 5 when you learned about witnessing to the world and reproducing believers, you focused on Christ's command to follow Him. This week you will focus on the commitment to cross bearing.

For Jesus, the cross meant that He gave Himself to redeem the world. For believers, cross bearing is voluntary, redemptive, sacrificial service for others. You enter His ministry by taking up your cross.

*" 'I tell you the truth, unless a kernel of wheat falls to the ground and dies, it remains only a single seed. But if it dies, it produces many seeds' " (John 12:24).*

**Read John 12:24 in the margin. Check the statement that best explains Jesus' comparison.**
❏ 1. Death to the old way of life brings forth new life.
❏ 2. Dying to self means that you will probably live your life alone.

You must die to your old way of life before you can commit yourself to Christ. Self-denial emphasizes turning from commitment to self to commitment to Him. Taking up your cross involves turning with Christ to the world in need. The first result is a new vision of self; the second result is a new vision of the world's need. The correct answer is 1.

*" 'Anyone who does not carry his cross and follow me cannot be my disciple' " (Luke 14:27).*

**Read Luke 14:27 in the margin. What happens to a person who refuses to be a cross bearer?**

_____

If you refuse to be a cross bearer, you cannot be Jesus' disciple. To follow Christ, you must bear your cross.

In Philippians 2:8, in the margin, Paul explained why Jesus was willing to take up His cross. Jesus was obedient to God's will for His life even when it meant dying on a cross. We learn from Jesus' example in

*Being found in appearance as a man,*
*he humbled himself*
*and became obedient to death—*
*even death on a cross!*
*(Phil. 2:8).*

cross bearing that a Christian's cross has two characteristics: (1) it is a voluntary commitment, and (2) it is an act of obedience.

**If you fail to take up your cross, which of the following sins have you committed?** ❑ **disobedience** ❑ **disloyalty** ❑ **disbelief**

Disloyalty and disbelief may be involved, but you are disobedient to Christ if you fail to take up your cross, because cross bearing is a direct command of Christ. Obeying Jesus' commands is the primary motive for taking up your cross. This week's Scripture-memory verse, John 15:13, states the value Jesus placed on sacrificial service to others.

 **Begin to memorize this week's Scripture-memory verse, John 15:13. Read it aloud. What did Jesus say that a disciple would be willing to do to demonstrate love for others?**

_____

Jesus said that a disciple ministers to others, even if you have to experience hardship or give your life.

## LEARNING THE DISCIPLE'S CROSS
The final addition to the cross will indicate how you relate to the world if you are Christ's disciple. If Christ is at the center of your life, you grow as His disciple through the discipline of ministering to others. As you grow in Christ, you reach out to others through service of all kinds. You bear Christ's cross even if it means experiencing difficulty.

 **Draw the Disciple's Cross over this picture of the world to show how a disciple reaches out to the world in witness and ministry. Label each part of the cross.**

**A disciple ministers to others, even if you have to experience hardship or give your life.**

DAILY MASTER
COMMUNICATION
GUIDE

LUKE 10:26-35

**What God said to me:**

_____

_____

_____

_____

_____

_____

**What I said to God:**

_____

_____

_____

_____

_____

_____

_____

_____

 Read Luke 10:26-35, a passage about someone who took up his cross for others, during your quiet time today. After you have read this passage, complete the Daily Master Communication Guide in the margin.

## DAY 2

# Ministry in Christ's Name

When I was the president of the Indonesian Baptist Theological Seminary, I hired a former lieutenant colonel in the Indonesian Army to manage the seminary property and the employees who took care of it. Although he had been a Christian for only about six months, he was very committed to the Lord. The problem was that he tried to manage the seminary property and employees as he would manage an army. Time after time I had to intervene to keep war from breaking out between the employees and this supervisor.

Praying for God's guidance, I decided to bear the cross and take on the difficulties required to disciple this man and to teach him to be an effective manager. Using the Scriptures, I taught him how to relate to his employees with patience, kindness, and self-control. This man effectively served at the seminary for more than 10 years.

Throughout your study of _MasterLife_ you have learned six biblical disciplines of a follower of Christ. In these disciplines four resources can be identified that are available to every disciple:
- the Word
- prayer
- fellowship
- witness

A growing disciple uses these four resources to help others in Christ's name. Your service expresses itself in various ministries:

> **1. The Word leads to a ministry of teaching/preaching.**
> 2. Prayer leads to a ministry of worship/intercession.
> 3. Fellowship leads to a ministry of nurture.
> 4. Witness leads to a ministry of evangelism.
> 5. Fellowship and witness lead to a ministry of service.

### A MINISTRY OF TEACHING/PREACHING
Look at the first ministry you will learn about, which appears in bold type in the box above. You may instantly think: _That lets me out. I'm not called to be a pastor. How can I minister this way?_

Preaching a sermon is certainly one way to minister by using the discipline of living in the Word. God definitely calls some people to be preachers or evangelists. If you live in the Word, you may learn that this role is His will for you. But you can be involved in the ministry of teaching or preaching even if you never proclaim the gospel in front of a congregation. Most people who stay in the Word long enough have the opportunity to share in a variety of contexts what God has said to them.

**Recall my story about the lieutenant colonel at the seminary. How did I use the resource of the Word in the ministry of teaching or preaching?**

**You can be involved in the ministry of teaching or preaching even if you never proclaim the gospel in front of a congregation.**

_____

_____

I used the resource of the Word to teach this man how the Lord wanted him to relate to his employees. By sharing with him what the Word says about patience, kindness, and self-control as fruit of the Spirit, I helped him manage in a more Christ-honoring manner.

**To understand how to use the resource of the Word in a ministry of teaching/preaching, you can look at ways teaching occurs in the Bible. Match the Scriptures in the margin with the following examples.**

___ 1. Job 36:22    a. **God is a teaching God. Many prophets such as Samuel also functioned as teachers.**

___ 2. Matthew 28:19    b. **Parents are urged to tell their children about God's mighty acts and to instruct them in God's commandments.**

___ 3. Ephesians 6:4    c. **In Jesus' ministry, teaching was His primary identity. In the Great Commission Jesus commanded His followers to make disciples and to instruct them in His teachings.**

___ 4. 1 Timothy 5:17    d. **Whenever new churches were founded, Christian teachers were present.**

*"God is exalted in his power. Who is a teacher like him?"* (Job 36:22).

*" 'Go and make disciples of all nations, baptizing them in the name of the Father and of the Son and of the Holy Spirit, and teaching them to obey everything I have commanded you' "* (Matt. 28:19).

*"Fathers, do not exasperate your children; instead, bring them up in the training and instruction of the Lord"* (Eph. 6:4).

*"The elders who direct the affairs of the church well are worthy of double honor, especially those whose work is preaching and teaching"* (1 Tim. 5:17).

Today teaching is part of sharing your faith. To witness to the world, believers must first understand the gospel and then teach others. A person can be involved in a teaching ministry whether from the pulpit, in a classroom, in a small-group study, or one-to-one. The correct answers are 1. a, 2. c, 3. b, 4. d.

## DAILY MASTER COMMUNICATION GUIDE

JOHN 17:6-19

**What God said to me:**

_____

_____

_____

_____

_____

_____

_____

**What I said to God:**

_____

_____

_____

_____

_____

_____

_____

_____

**Name ways you might be able to use the resource of the Word in a ministry of teaching or preaching.**

_____

_____

Do not feel concerned if ideas for ministry do not immediately occur to you. The goal is to open new possibilities for you as you begin considering your ministry as a follower of Christ.

Memorizing Scripture is one way you can begin to use the resource of the Word. When you hide God's Word in your heart, you have it at instant recall when you want to share about Christ or to give scriptural guidance or encouragement.

 **By now you have likely memorized six verses and are working on a seventh one. On a sheet of paper, see how accurately you can write each of the six by memory.**

If you had difficulty writing any of the six verses, you may want to review "How to Memorize Scripture" in week 5.

**Continue your work on this week's Scripture-memory verse, John 15:13. Say it aloud from one to three times. Ask a family member or someone you see each day if you can practice saying it aloud to him or her.**

A MINISTRY OF WORSHIP/INTERCESSION
The ministry in bold type below is the next one you will study.

> 1. The Word leads to a ministry of teaching/preaching.
> **2. Prayer leads to a ministry of worship/intercession.**
> 3. Fellowship leads to a ministry of nurture.
> 4. Witness leads to a ministry of evangelism.
> 5. Fellowship and witness lead to a ministry of service.

The more you get involved in prayer, the more you worship. Prayer is ministering before the Lord (see 1 Chron. 23:13). It is bowing before God and worshiping Him through praise, adoration, and devotion. Prayer enables you to develop a closer relationship with the Father. Intercession is a way you can minister to others by bringing their needs before God.

The ministry of worship can take the form of individual worship during your quiet time. But it goes beyond private prayer. You also worship as you fellowship with the body of Christ, gathered as His church. Worship as a church family has occurred since the time of the first Christians. Read the verses from Acts in the margin on the next page.

Again, you may think: *I'm not a minister or a church-staff member. How can I perform a ministry of worship?* The focus of true worship is on God and your personal relationship with Him. If you never lead others in worship, you can serve the Lord through worship. He waits for your worship. Worship is the primary way you glorify the Lord and is God's primary reason for creating and redeeming you (see 1 Pet. 2:9). The early church did not limit leadership in worship to professional ministers. Everyone has a responsibility for worship, whether God provides opportunities to lead groups in worship experiences or to participate in worship by following others' directions. We can also worship in our families as we minister to the persons closest to us. Read Deuteronomy 6:6-9 in the margin.

As you learned in week 4, intercession is a disciple's ministry to bring to God the needs of the church and the world. Intercession can result in changed lives and changed churches. Staying alert to persons' needs and jotting down their concerns allow you to intercede for them as you pray individually or with others.

**How do you think God wants you to use the resource of prayer in a ministry of worship and intercession?**

_____

_____

You can start by interceding for believers who serve the Lord by spreading the gospel throughout the world. Pray for them as they witness to the world and as they lead others to witness. Become a prayer partner with them. Let them know that you are praying for them and that they can depend on your prayers. You may want to add the names of your pastor and other church-staff members to your Prayer-Covenant List and to pray for their specific needs.

Before I became a missionary, I heard many missionaries say that their greatest need was prayer, even more than finances. I made a commitment to God that before I began to serve as a missionary, I would enlist as many prayer partners as possible so that He could do more than I could do as a missionary. I enlisted about two thousand people to pray daily. Over the years that list grew to six thousand. I wrote to them every month to give them prayer requests and to report answers to prayer. I believe that God's work through us in Indonesia was a direct answer to those prayer partners' prayers. Think about what God could do through your pastor and church-staff members if you and others regularly prayed for them!

Stop now and pray for your pastor and church-staff members by name. Pray for the other members of your church who serve in the areas of teaching, prayer, outreach, benev-

*"They devoted themselves to the apostles' teaching and to the fellowship, to the breaking of bread and to prayer. Every day they continued to meet together in the temple courts. They broke bread in their homes and ate together with glad and sincere hearts" (Acts 2:42,46).*

*" 'These commandments that I give to you today are to be upon your hearts. Impress them on your children. Talk about them when you sit at home and when you walk along the road, when you lie down and when you get up. Tie them as symbols on your hands and bind them on your foreheads. Write them on the doorframes of your houses and on your gates' " (Deut. 6:6-9).*

olence, missions, music, and others. Ask God to bless each person as he or she ministers to others. Ask Him to help you think of ways you can support and demonstrate love for your church leaders.

Read John 17:6-19 during your quiet time today. Let God speak to you through this passage about Jesus' intercession for His disciples. After you have read this passage, complete the Daily Master Communication Guide on page 120.

## DAY 3
# More Ways to Minister

You have already studied two ministries and the resources that lead to their expression in the life of a disciple. Now you will learn a third, listed in bold type with its corresponding resource.

> 1. The Word leads to a ministry of teaching/preaching.
> 2. Prayer leads to a ministry of worship/intercession.
> **3. Fellowship leads to a ministry of nurture.**
> 4. Witness leads to a ministry of evangelism.
> 5. Fellowship and witness lead to a ministry of service.

### A MINISTRY OF NURTURE
Fellowshipping with believers eventually leads you to disciple new Christians. A normal outgrowth of being part of the body of Christ is taking care of spiritual infants and helping them grow into mature Christians. God gives some persons special gifts to counsel and train others in the various stages of spiritual growth. In the Bible this happens several times, as when Jesus saw Simon's potential and helped him grow into the rock called Peter (see John 21:15-17 in the margin). Barnabas encouraged the reluctant John Mark, who grew and later wrote one of the Gospels. Christ will show you Himself as you fellowship with other believers.

A ministry of nurture could involve—
❑ counseling new Christians at the time of decision;
❑ helping spiritual infants understand what it means to have life in Christ;
❑ leading a small group of disciples to know what following Christ means;
❑ serving on committees that see potential in members and recommending them for church offices;
❑ training leaders;

*"When they had finished eating, Jesus said to Simon Peter, 'Simon, son of John, do you truly love me more than these?' 'Yes, Lord,' he said, 'you know that I love you.' Jesus said, 'Feed my lambs.' Again Jesus said, 'Simon, son of John, do you truly love me?' He answered, 'Yes, Lord, you know that I love you.' Jesus said, 'Take care of my sheep.' The third time he said to him, 'Simon, son of John, do you love me?' Peter was hurt because Jesus asked him the third time, 'Do you love me?' He said, 'Lord, you know all things; you know that I love you.' Jesus said, 'Feed my sheep' "
(John 21:15-17).*

❏ teaching persons how to witness;
❏ counseling persons about their interpersonal needs.

In all situations nurture can involve role modeling, as Christ did with those He trained as His disciples. Others need examples of the Christian life that point them to Christ.

**In the previous list, check the ways you already serve and draw a star beside the one(s) you think God might want you to do in a ministry of nurture.**

Remember the definition of *discipleship* you learned earlier? Now read this definition of *discipling*, or *making disciples*.

> Discipling is leading others to develop personal, lifelong, obedient relationships with Christ in which He transforms their character into Christlikeness, changes their values to Kingdom values, and involves them in His mission.

To carry out the Great Commission, you need to lead others into lifelong, obedient relationships with Jesus Christ. That is your responsibility. Then help them grow in their relationships with Him until He transforms them into His likeness and involves them in His mission. Every disciple is to help other disciples in the fellowship of believers grow.

Do you think you have been a role model for others during your study of *MasterLife*? Has anyone made a comment to you like "You seem to have changed since you began this study"? If so, perhaps this has occurred because of an increased understanding of what it means to live the Christian life. Maybe someone has observed you reaching out to nurture others as you have had fellowship with believers. Perhaps your family members have observed you having a quiet time. I hope that your lifestyle has changed to the point that new ways of thinking and behaving are obvious.

**Every disciple is to help other disciples in the fellowship of believers grow.**

 **Tell someone how you have benefited from your study of** *MasterLife*. **Do this regardless of whether someone has commented about having observed changes in your life.**

## A MINISTRY OF EVANGELISM
The fourth ministry of a disciple appears in bold type below.

> 1. The Word leads to a ministry of teaching/preaching.
> 2. Prayer leads to a ministry of worship/intercession.
> 3. Fellowship leads to a ministry of nurture.
> **4. Witness leads to a ministry of evangelism.**
> 5. Fellowship and witness lead to a ministry of service.

The well-known evangelist D. L. Moody had a personal commitment

**All evangelism starts with personal witness.**

that he would witness to someone every day of his life. Even if he had already gone to bed when he remembered that he had not witnessed that day, he would get up and tell someone about Christ.[1] The final resource you have for living the Christian life is the resource of witness. Many believers do not think of witness as a resource. However, nothing encourages Christians more than bearing witness, especially when they see someone accept Christ. From the resource of witness grows a ministry of evangelism. Various types of evangelism exist—film evangelism, relational evangelism, tracts, crusades—but all start with personal witness.

Evangelism is the proclamation of the good news of salvation in Christ. Our evangelism is a means the Holy Spirit uses to convert the lost. It is the way the Lord uses us to teach others about Himself. As a Christian, you do not persuade persons simply to make decisions. Rather, you tell them about Christ, call them to repentance, and give God the glory for what occurs.

**Read the Great Commission, Matthew 28:19, in the margin. What does Christ say about your responsibility for evangelism?**

_____

_____

*" 'Go and make disciples of all nations, baptizing them in the name of the Father and of the Son and of the Holy Spirit, and teaching them to obey everything I have commanded you' " (Matt. 28:19).*

The Great Commission calls you to use the resource of witness. Through the Great Commission Christ gave you the responsibility to share with others your knowledge of His love.

You may think: *How do I do this? I'm not a D. L. Moody. I'm not a Billy Graham. I don't have the abilities of a TV evangelist or someone who draws large crowds to tell about Christ.* Remember that D. L. Moody used the resource of witness to deal with one person at a time long before he became a preaching evangelist. Personal witness is a significant way to express the ministry of evangelism.

 **Write your memory verse, John 15:13, in the margin. Describe here what you think a person who is willing to give his or her life for a friend would do about witnessing.**

_____

_____

You may have said that a person who would give everything for a friend would make sure that person has the gift of eternal life by witnessing to friends.

You can express this ministry of evangelism in a variety of ways:
❏ Lifestyle—living a Christian life that attracts a lost person's attention

and provides an opportunity for witness

❑ Small-group evangelism—participating in small groups of persons with similar interests to share the gospel of Christ

❑ Church evangelism—visiting homes, taking a religious census, or using other actions to ensure that every person in your church's range of influence hears the gospel message

❑ Mass evangelism—helping your church gather people for a community-wide revival in a church building or a stadium

❑ Missions ministry—entering other cultures to tell others about Jesus as a career, short-term, or bivocational missionary or through giving and praying for missions causes

❑ Other: _____

**In the previous list, check the ways you have already served and draw a star beside the one(s) you think God might want you to do in a ministry of evangelism.**

At this point you may not know exactly how God intends for you to minister in this area. The purpose of these exercises is to encourage you to begin thinking of ways you can use the valuable resources that are yours as a disciple of Christ.

## LEARNING THE DISCIPLE'S CROSS

**Again draw the Disciple's Cross over the picture of the world. Then add pointed arrows to the ends of the cross-bars. At the ends of the pointed arrows write the ministry areas that go with each part of the cross:** *ministry of teaching/preaching* **below the cross,** *ministry of worship/intercession* **above the cross,** *ministry of nurture* **to the right of the cross, and** *ministry of evangelism* **to the left of the cross.**

Read 1 Timothy 6:11-21 in your quiet time today. Let God speak to you through this passage about the way Paul nurtured Timothy. After you have read this passage, complete the Daily Master Communication Guide in the margin on page 125.

# DAY 4

## The Demands of Christ

Jesus did not always paint a rosy picture for the disciples as He talked about what was ahead for them. During His last days on earth Jesus outlined for His disciples what they could expect if they followed Him. Any suffering they would encounter for taking up His cross would be sorrow He had already known. In the verse in the margin He told them that the world would hate them because they were associated with Him and because they would witness in His name. Sometimes you may be inclined to skip over verses like John 15:18 because they indicate that life in Christ will be difficult. Read what an Argentine pastor says about this subject:

*" 'If the world hates you, keep in mind that it hated me first' " (John 15:18).*

> The gospel which we have in the Bible is the gospel of the Kingdom of God. It presents Jesus as King, as Lord, as the maximum authority. Jesus is at the very center. The gospel of the Kingdom is a Christ-centered gospel.
>
> But in recent centuries we have been hearing another gospel—a man-centered, human gospel. It is the gospel of the big offer. The gospel of the hot sale. The gospel of the irresistible special deal. ... We have told people, "If you accept Jesus, you will have joy, you will have peace, health, prosperity. ... If you give Jesus ten dollars, you will get twenty dollars back." ... We are always appealing to man's interests. Jesus is the Savior, the Healer, and the King coming for me. Me is the center of our gospel.
>
> We take all the verses we like, all the verses that offer something or promise something—John 3:16, John 5:24, and so forth—and we make a systematic theology from these verses, while we forget the other verses that present the demands of Jesus Christ. ... Who said we were allowed to present only one side of Jesus? ... He is our Savior and our Healer, true. But we cannot cut Jesus Christ into pieces and take only the piece we like best.[2]

**We cannot accept the part of Jesus' message that we like and reject what we do not like. We must accept it all.**

We cannot accept the part of Jesus' message that we like and reject what we do not like. We must accept it all.

**List commands Christ gave for disciples that you have ignored.**

_____

_____

_____

## EXPECT TO BE REJECTED

The reality is, when you meet the demands of Christ as you minister to others, you may experience rejection. For example, did you feel rejection or sense a lack of openness to you as you began reaching out to your new non-Christian friend? Sometimes you may feel subtle rejection at first. Or you may initially sense that your friend would not be open to eventually learning about Christ.

One of my neighbors who was not a Christian began to play on the church softball team I played on. I tried to share my faith tactfully with him as we became better acquainted, but I never felt that he was ready to respond. I could not help feeling somewhat rejected when I continually sensed that he was not open to my witness.

One day as I was preparing to go overseas to lead _MasterLife_ training, I sensed God leading me to talk to my neighbor before I left. That night my wife and I visited him and led him to Christ. Befriending him and regularly expressing concern for him eventually provided a witnessing opportunity. I was glad I had not become discouraged when at first I felt somewhat rejected.

**This week do something kind for the non-Christian friend you made last week. Learn all you can about your new friend. Be ready to tell your _MasterLife_ group what happened.**

## THE PROMISE OF HIS PRESENCE

After warning His disciples about the possibility of rejection, however, Jesus painted another picture designed to compel them to spread the good news fervently regardless of what they encountered. Read the verses in the margin.

Jesus reassured the disciples that they would have the Holy Spirit to assist them as they testified about Christ. He would not leave them without help or resources. The Holy Spirit would guide them as they moved out to serve others.

Two thousand years later, Jesus makes the same promise to you and gives you the same commands. As He sends you out to serve the world that He warns will hate you, He does not leave you without resources. He gives you the Holy Spirit to empower you and to make you bold.

**When you meet the demands of Christ, you may experience rejection.**

_" 'When the Counselor comes, whom I will send to you from the Father, the Spirit of truth who goes out from the Father, he will testify about me. And you also must testify, for you have been with me from the beginning' " (John 15:26-27)._

Pray for the lost persons the group members mentioned at the previous session. You may have written their names on your Prayer-Covenant List or elsewhere. If you did not, you may want to add their names at the next group session. Meanwhile, continue praying that your fellow *MasterLife* group members will live Christlike lives that will model Christ to others.

**Your witness and your fellowship involve Christian service to other persons.**

A MINISTRY OF SERVICE

Could a ministry of service be the ministry to which Christ calls you? Your witness and your fellowship involve Christian service to other persons. These compose the fifth ministry area to add to the four you have already studied.

> 1. The Word leads to a ministry of teaching/preaching.
> 2. Prayer leads to a ministry of worship/intercession.
> 3. Fellowship leads to a ministry of nurture.
> 4. Witness leads to a ministry of evangelism.
> **5. Fellowship and witness lead to a ministry of service.**

John 15:13 says, " 'Greater love has no one than this, that he lay down his life for his friends.' " You are to be involved in a ministry of service as Christ was.

LEARNING THE DISCIPLE'S CROSS

Draw the Disciple's Cross as you learned to do in day 3, with the cross over the world and with the pointed arrows on the crossbars. Label the ministry areas. Then write *ministry of service, John 15:13* above the horizontal crossbar. As you label it with the disciplines, ministries, and Scriptures that accompany it, explain it aloud. Be sure to say aloud all of the memory verses you recorded on it.

A Growing Disciples Workshop will conclude this study. At this workshop you will review what you have learned and will prepare to begin *MasterLife 2: The Disciple's Personality.* Before the workshop share the Disciple's Cross with a member of your group.

WHAT IT MEANS TO BE A DISCIPLE
You can learn an easy way to remember what you have studied in book 1 of *MasterLife*. Summarizing what it means to be a disciple is as simple as 1-2-3-4-5-6:

**1 Lord as the first priority of your life**
• The center of the cross emphasizes spending time with the Master.

**2 relationships**
• The vertical crossbar represents your relationship with God.
• The horizontal crossbar represents your relationship with others.

**3 commitments**
• Deny yourself
• Take up your cross
• Follow Christ

**4 resources to center your life in Christ**
• The Word
• Prayer
• Fellowship
• Witness

**5 ministries that grow from the four resources**
• Teaching/preaching
• Worship/intercession
• Nurture
• Evangelism
• Service

**6 disciplines of a disciple**
• Spend time with the Master
• Live in the Word
• Pray in faith
• Fellowship with believers
• Witness to the world
• Minister to others

**1 Lord**
**2 relationships**
**3 commitments**
**4 resources**
**5 ministries**
**6 disciplines**

To reinforce this 1-2-3-4-5-6 plan for discipleship, **fill in the blanks that follow.**

**A disciple of Christ has—**

1 _____.

## DAILY MASTER COMMUNICATION GUIDE

### JOHN 15

**What God said to me:**

_____

_____

_____

_____

_____

_____

_____

**What I said to God:**

_____

_____

_____

_____

_____

_____

_____

2 relationships: _____.

3 commitments: _____
_____.

4 resources: _____
_____.

5 ministries: _____
_____
_____.

6 disciplines: _____
_____
_____
_____.

Again read John 15 in your quiet time today. This time look for ways God speaks to you through this passage about ministering to others. After you have read this passage, complete the Daily Master Communication Guide in the margin.

Are your daily quiet times making a difference in your life? Are you interceding for others? Are you gaining strength? Has your quiet time raised your entire walk with the Lord to a different level? If so, draw a star in the blank here: _____.

Everything you have done in your study of *MasterLife 1: The Disciple's Cross,* including memorizing seven Scriptures and learning the Disciple's Cross, has required quite a time commitment. I pray that you have found this commitment worthwhile. I hope that by improving the use of your time through the MasterTime concept, you have found time to commit to tasks the Lord has in mind for you. I hope that the MasterTime form is becoming a regular part of your life.

Stop and pray, asking God to continue to lead you as you plan your time, using the MasterTime form. Be ready to share with your group how your planning has benefited from using MasterTime.

HAS THIS WEEK MADE A DIFFERENCE?
Review "My Walk with the Master This Week." Mark the activities you have finished and finish the ones you have not completed. Then look back through all of book 1. Finish any activities from previous weeks that you may not have completed. Consider what you will report during the Growing Disciples Workshop about what these activities have meant to you.

# DAY 5

## A Disciple Indeed

In 1983 I led *MasterLife* training in Kenya after almost being denied access to the country. Four years earlier when Communists had taken control of Ethiopia, they had banned worship in churches by ordering that no more than five persons could meet at any time without a permit. Naturally, the Communists did not grant permission for worship services. An Ethiopian Christian I met at the training said that many members of his eight-hundred-member church became backsliders in their faith because circumstances were so difficult.

"Seven other men and I decided that we must do something to carry on the work," he told me. They approached missionary veterinarian Jerry Bedsole, who was allowed to stay in Ethiopia because he took care of the animals at the palace. Jerry began to disciple these Ethiopian Christians secretly at his house, using *MasterLife*. Later, each man discipled four persons. "We could not meet at the same place or time each week; we could not take Bibles to a meeting; and we had to pray with our eyes open, using conversational prayer, so that we would not be discovered," the man said.

Because the Ethiopian Christians feared that the Communists would soon confiscate their Bibles, they devised a plan for each person to memorize a part of the Bible so that they could reproduce it. "I'm memorizing one of the Gospels," he told me.

"Oh, yes, we know we will be put in jail. Some of us already have been, but the government doesn't know what to do with us once we are behind bars. We witness and win the other prisoners, so they soon kick us out," he said. Eventually, my friend began underground discipleship groups in 170 places around the country.

Several years later, after the Communists were overthrown, my Ethiopian friend was visiting Kenya when I returned there. This irrepressible man was still on fire for Christ—this time without an oppressive government to restrain him. He reported that the churches of Ethiopia had just purchased one hundred thousand sets of *MasterLife* to train Ethiopians to be disciples.

When the door seems to be closed, God can make a way for us to serve Him. Often, we must adjust our lives to follow Him in obedience.

**What if you did not have a church in which to worship? What would you do if you could not sing praises to God? What if a government took away your Bible to prohibit your witness? Describe how you would stay connected to the Vine.**

**"We must do something to carry on the work."**

**When the door seems to be closed, God can make a way for us to serve Him.**

**The Disciple's Cross represents your relationship with Christ as His disciple.**

I hope that as you have studied *MasterLife 1: The Disciple's Cross,* your relationship with Christ has become so important to you that you would bear your cross in any way possible to obey Christ.

LEARNING THE DISCIPLE'S CROSS
The Disciple's Cross has been the basis for impromptu sermons, conversations, and witnessing opportunities by persons who learned it and mastered its concepts. I hope that for you, however, the cross represents something even greater. It represents your relationship with Christ as His disciple. I hope that by this point in your study, the Disciple's Cross is at the very core of your being—that it is a way of life for you. I hope that spending time with the Master, praying in faith, living in the Word, fellowshipping with believers, witnessing to the world, and ministering to others are becoming disciplines you use every day to live in Christ.

If the Disciple's Cross is a part of your life—

❑ you will know six biblical disciplines of a disciple;
❑ you will experience a closer relationship with Christ as you practice the disciplines each day;
❑ you will use the Disciple's Cross as the standard to remind yourself and other Christians of the commitments required for being Christ's disciple;
❑ you will use the six disciplines to follow the Holy Spirit's direction as you confront problems;
❑ you will help other disciples live in Christ and bear fruit for His glory.

*"If a man cleanses himself from the latter, he will be an instrument for noble purposes, made holy, useful to the Master and prepared to do any good work" (2 Tim. 2:21).*

Your goal in discipleship is expressed in 2 Timothy 2:21, in the margin. Grow in all of the disciplines to master life and be prepared for the Master's use. If you develop all of these disciplines, your life will be balanced and fruitful.

**Review the above list of ways that knowing the Disciple's Cross can help you as a disciple. Check the ways you are already benefiting from knowing the Disciple's Cross. Then draw a star beside ways you hope to continue growing in your use of the Disciple's Cross.**

You learned the six disciplines by using a diagram of a cross. One way to reinforce the fact that you have learned these disciplines is to illustrate them in another form. Think about another item—a car, a tree, a mountain, a building, an ice-cream cone, or another object—you can draw to illustrate the elements of the Disciple's Cross. Perhaps you feel that you do not have artistic ability. Do not worry about how the final product looks; the most important point is to include all of the concepts.

Draw the alternative item you have chosen to illustrate the disciplines. Include the memory verses that go with them. If you need more room, use a blank sheet of paper. When you finish, insert the sheet in your book at this place. Be prepared to explain your illustration at the Growing Disciples Workshop.

 Read 2 Timothy 2 during your quiet time and complete the Daily Master Communication Guide in the margin.

WHERE ARE YOU IN YOUR RELATIONSHIP WITH CHRIST?
How equipped are you to be Christ's disciple? The Growing Disciples Workshop that follows this study will help you determine the answer. Before you attend the workshop, complete the Discipleship Inventory on pages 139–43 to evaluate your growth in discipleship. The inventory, based on the characteristics of a disciple, can help you determine where you are in your growth as a disciple. Even though the inventory will help you look at yourself in terms of behavior and attitudes, the most important questions you can ask yourself are: *Where am I in my relationship with Christ? How far am I from the lifelong, obedient relationship with Him that I desire? If He desires to transform my values into Kingdom values, have I arrived?*

When you attend the Growing Disciples Workshop, you will learn how to interpret your answers. At this point you may decide that you need to do additional work in certain areas of your relationship with Christ. You will take this inventory again at the end of book 4 to identify the areas in which you have grown.

Congratulations on completing *MasterLife 1: The Disciple's Cross.* I hope that you are beginning to learn what being a follower of Christ means. But the pilgrimage has just begun. I encourage you to study *MasterLife 2: The Disciple's Personality* to continue the journey of your lifelong, obedient relationship with your Savior and Lord, Jesus Christ.

---

[1]R. A. Torrey, *Why God Used D. L. Moody* (Chicago: Moody Press, 1923), 42.
[2]Juan Carlos Ortiz, *Disciple* (Carol Stream, Ill.: Creation House, 1975), 12–16.

## DAILY MASTER COMMUNICATION GUIDE
### 2 TIMOTHY 2

**What God said to me:**

_____

_____

_____

_____

_____

_____

_____

**What I said to God:**

_____

_____

_____

_____

_____

_____

_____

_____

# The Disciple's Cross

The Disciple's Cross is the focal point for all you learn in *MasterLife 1: The Disciple's Cross*. The cross provides an instrument for visualizing and understanding your opportunities and responsibilities as a disciple of Christ.

Following are step-by-step instructions for presenting the Disciple's Cross to another person. Each week of this study you learn a portion of the Disciple's Cross and the Scripture that accompanies it. As you learn the cross and review it in the future, you may find it helpful to refer to this step-by-step explanation and to the completed drawing on page 136. Do not attempt to memorize this presentation. You will learn how to present it in your own words. Do not feel overwhelmed by the amount of material involved. You will learn it in weekly segments. By the end of the study you will be able to explain the entire cross and to say all of the verses that accompany it.

To explain the cross to someone, use a blank, unlined sheet of paper to draw the illustration developed here in stages. Instructions to you are in parentheses. The following material is the presentation you make to the other person.

A disciple of Christ is a person who makes Christ the Lord of his or her life. (Quote Luke 9:23 and write the reference and the three commitments in the upper right corner of the page: *deny, cross, follow.*) A disciple's first commitment is to deny yourself. That does not mean to reject your identity but to renounce the self-centered life. To do that, a disciple of Christ learns the following six disciplines of the Christian life.

## SPEND TIME WITH THE MASTER
(In the center of the page draw a circle.) The empty circle represents your life. It pictures denying all of self for Christ. You cannot be a disciple of Christ if you are not willing to deny self. If this circle represents your life, Christ should fill the entire circle as you focus on Him. (Write the word *Christ* in the circle.) Christ is to have priority in everything. Life in Christ is Christ living in you.

(Write *John 15:5* under the word *Christ* in the circle and quote the verse from memory.) What can you do without abiding in Christ? Nothing! Christ said that He is the Vine and that we are the branches. The branches are part of the Vine. You are part of Christ. He wants to live His life through you. Is this the kind of life you would like to have?

**Luke 9:23**
**Deny**
**Cross**
**Follow**

**Christ**
John 15:5

In addition to denying yourself, you need to take up your cross. The Disciple's Cross pictures the resources Christ gives us to help us live in Him. (Draw the cross around the circle.)

## LIVE IN THE WORD
The way to have life in Christ is to have His Word in you. (Write *Word* and *John 8:31-32* on the lower crossbar and quote these verses from memory.) The Word is your food. You cannot grow closer to Christ unless you regularly partake of the Word. You receive the Word in many ways: by listening to someone preach it, by reading it, by studying it, by memorizing it, by meditating on it, and by applying it. Making Christ Lord means that you want to study, meditate on, and apply the Word regularly.

## PRAY IN FAITH
Part of life in Christ and of having a relationship with Him is praying in faith. (Write *prayer* and *John 15:7* on the upper crossbar and quote the verse from memory. Point to the words *Christ*, *Word*, and *prayer* as you quote the corresponding parts of the verse.) If you

abide in Christ and His Word abides in you, you can ask what you want, and God will do it. Notice that the vertical bar of the cross, representing the Word and prayer, highlights your relationship with God, the basic ways you communicate with God, and the basic ways He communicates with you.

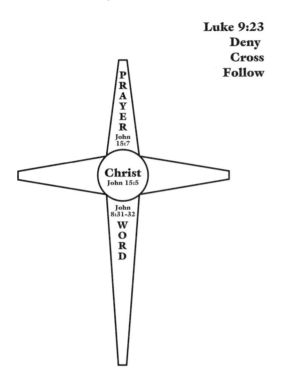

**Luke 9:23**
**Deny**
**Cross**
**Follow**

## FELLOWSHIP WITH BELIEVERS

Life in Christ means that you live in fellowship with your brothers and sisters in Christ. (Write *fellowship* and *John 13:34-35* on the right crossbar and quote these verses from memory.) Jesus said the way to show that you are His disciple is to love one another. God provided the ideal place for you to grow—His church. A church is not a building or an organization, although it uses both of these. A church is a body of baptized believers who have agreed to carry out Christ's ministry in the world. A committed Christian stays in fellowship with a local body of believers in order to grow in Christ. The church is the body of Christ! If you have life in Christ, you realize how important living in His body, the church, is.

## WITNESS TO THE WORLD

Life in Christ includes witnessing to others. It involves following Him, another commitment of a disciple. Witnessing is sharing with others about Christ and

your relationship with Him. (Write *witness* and *John 15:8* on the left crossbar and quote the verse from memory.) If you abide in Christ, you eventually bear fruit. Fruit can be the fruit of the Spirit or a new Christian. Ephesians 5:22-23 lists the fruit of the Spirit as love, joy, peace, patience, kindness, goodness, faithfulness, gentleness, and self-control. Fruit does not always grow quickly, but it grows continually and bears in season. Fruit bearing is the normal, natural result when you have Christ at the center of your life.

Jesus said the way to show that you are His disciple is to bear much fruit. This includes witnessing. Witnessing is the natural outgrowth of living in Christ. If you are spending time with the Master, living daily in the Word, praying in faith, and fellowshipping with God's people, you naturally share with others the Christ who lives in your heart.

**Luke 9:23**
**Deny**
**Cross**
**Follow**

## MINISTER TO OTHERS

As the fruit of the Spirit grows in your life in Christ, you also reach out to others through ministry. You take up your cross in service to others, which is another commitment of a disciple. Cross bearing is voluntary, redemptive service for others.

Look again at the circle in the center of the cross. Your life in Christ should continue to grow and expand. (Make circular broken lines that move out from the center of the circle.)

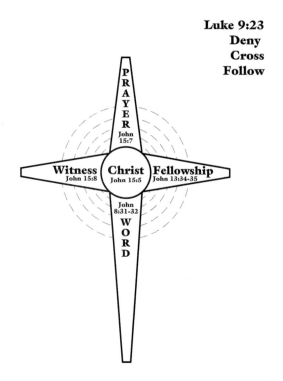

**Luke 9:23**
**Deny**
**Cross**
**Follow**

to do any good work." You need to grow in all spiritual disciplines and ministries to master life and to be prepared for the Master's use. If you develop all of these disciplines, your life will be balanced and fruitful.

(As you present the following, write the number and the first word following the number in the upper left corner of the page.) To remember this illustration, notice that you have—

1 Lord as the first priority of your life;
2 relationships: a vertical relationship with God and horizontal relationships with others;
3 commitments: deny self, take up your cross daily, and follow Christ;
4 resources to center your life in Christ: the Word, prayer, fellowship, and witness;
5 ministries that grow from the four resources: teaching/preaching, worship/intercession, nurture, evangelism, and service;
6 disciplines of a disciple: spend time with the Master, live in the Word, pray in faith, fellowship with believers, witness to the world, and minister to others.

As you grow in Christ, you reach out to others through all kinds of ministry and service. (Add pointed arrows to the ends of the crossbars.) The arrows indicate that your growth in Christ should express itself in ministries. Living in the Word leads to a ministry of teaching or preaching. (Write *ministry of teaching/preaching* below the cross.)

Praying in faith leads to a ministry of worship or intercession. (Write *ministry of worship/intercession* above the cross.)

Fellowshipping with believers leads to a ministry of nurture to other believers. (Write *ministry of nurture* to the right of the cross.)

Witnessing to the world leads to a ministry of evangelism. (Write *ministry of evangelism* to the left of the cross.)

Your witness and your fellowship lead to Christian service to other persons. (Write *ministry of service: John 15:13* above the horizontal bar and quote the verse.) Notice that the horizontal bar of the cross, representing witness and ministry, highlights your relationships with others.

These five ministry areas compose the ministry of a disciple and of Christ's church. The goal of discipleship is expressed in 2 Timothy 2:21: "If a man cleanses himself from the latter, he will be an instrument for noble purposes, made holy, useful to the Master and prepared

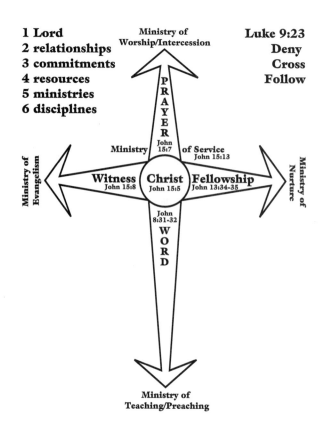

By practicing these biblical principles, you can abide in Christ and can be useful in the Master's service.

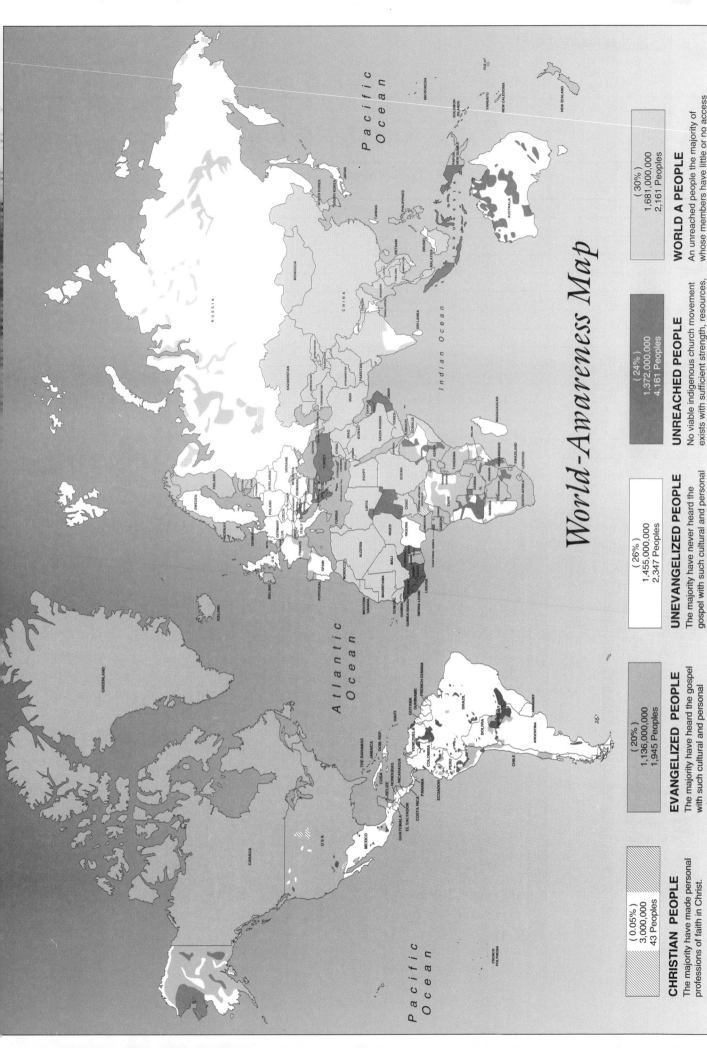

# World-Awareness Map

**CHRISTIAN PEOPLE**

( 0.05% )
3,000,000
43 Peoples

The majority have made personal professions of faith in Christ.

**EVANGELIZED PEOPLE**

( 20% )
1,136,000,000
1,945 Peoples

The majority have heard the gospel with such cultural and personal relevance that it results in sufficient understanding to accept Christ by faith or to reject Him.

**UNEVANGELIZED PEOPLE**

( 26% )
1,455,000,000
2,347 Peoples

The majority have never heard the gospel with such cultural and personal relevance that it results in sufficient understanding to accept Christ by faith or to reject Him.

**UNREACHED PEOPLE**

( 24% )
1,372,000,000
4,161 Peoples

No viable indigenous church movement exists with sufficient strength, resources, and commitment to sustain and ensure the continuous multiplication of churches.

**WORLD A PEOPLE**

( 30% )
1,681,000,000
2,161 Peoples

An unreached people the majority of whose members have little or no access to the gospel of Jesus Christ.

## Prayer-Covenant List

| Request | Date | Bible Promise | Answer | Date |
|---------|------|---------------|--------|------|
|  |  |  |  |  |
|  |  |  |  |  |
|  |  |  |  |  |
|  |  |  |  |  |
|  |  |  |  |  |
|  |  |  |  |  |
|  |  |  |  |  |
|  |  |  |  |  |
|  |  |  |  |  |
|  |  |  |  |  |
|  |  |  |  |  |
|  |  |  |  |  |
|  |  |  |  |  |
|  |  |  |  |  |
|  |  |  |  |  |
|  |  |  |  |  |
|  |  |  |  |  |
|  |  |  |  |  |
|  |  |  |  |  |

## MasterTime

Day _____ Date _____

Priority

Minutes

My Walk with the Master This Week Commitments

Planning Ahead

Work to Do

Telephone (Person, Subject, Number)

# Discipleship Inventory

This Discipleship Inventory[1] measures the functional discipleship level of individuals, groups, and churches. By using the inventory, believers can assess their development by considering 30 characteristics of a New Testament disciple in the categories of attitudes, behavior, relationships, ministry, and doctrine.

Follow these directions to complete the inventory:

- Respond to each statement as honestly as possible. Select an answer that most clearly reflects your life as it is, not as you would like it to be.
- Choose one answer for each statement.
- Note changes in the types of answers from section to section.
- Do not spend too much time on any one question.

You will receive instructions for scoring your inventory at the Growing Disciples Workshop that follows this study.

**How true is each of the following statements of you? Choose from these responses:**

    1 = never true    4 = often true
    2 = rarely true    5 = almost always true
    3 = sometimes true

1. I strive to live by the Bible's moral and ethical teachings. 1 2 3 4 5
2. Reading and studying the Bible has made significant changes in the way I live my life. 1 2 3 4 5
3. My faith shapes how I think and act each day. 1 2 3 4 5
4. I talk with other persons about my beliefs in Christ as Savior and Lord. 1 2 3 4 5
5. I take time for periods of prayer or meditation. 1 2 3 4 5
6. Because God has forgiven me, I respond with a forgiving attitude when others wrong me. 1 2 3 4 5
7. While interacting with others in everyday contacts, I seek opportunities to speak out about Jesus Christ. 1 2 3 4 5
8. My neighbors and the persons I work with know that I am a Christian. 1 2 3 4 5
9. I go out of my way to show love to persons I meet. 1 2 3 4 5
10. When I realize that I have disobeyed a specific teaching of the Bible, I correct the wrongdoing. 1 2 3 4 5
11. I pray for God's help when I have needs or problems. 1 2 3 4 5
12. I share personal feelings and needs with Christian friends. 1 2 3 4 5
13. I hold a grudge when treated unfairly. 1 2 3 4 5
14. I devote time to reading and studying the Bible. 1 2 3 4 5
15. I like to worship and pray with others. 1 2 3 4 5
16. I use my gifts and talents to serve others. 1 2 3 4 5
17. When I become aware that I have offended someone, I go to him or her to admit and correct my wrongdoing. 1 2 3 4 5
18. I pray for the salvation of friends and acquaintances who are not professing Christians. 1 2 3 4 5
19. I work to remove barriers or problems that develop between me and my friends. 1 2 3 4 5
20. I feel too inadequate to help others. 1 2 3 4 5

**How often, if ever, do you do each of the following? Choose from these responses:**

1 = seldom or never    4 = several times a week
2 = about once a month    5 = once a day or more
3 = about once a week

21. Pray with other Christians, other than during church 1 2 3 4 5
22. Participate in a small-group Bible study, other than Sunday School 1 2 3 4 5
23. Pray or meditate, other than at church or before meals 1 2 3 4 5
24. Memorize verses or passages of the Bible 1 2 3 4 5
25. Study the Bible on my own 1 2 3 4 5
26. Pray specifically for missions and missionaries 1 2 3 4 5

**Indicate how much you agree or disagree with each of the following statements. Choose from these responses:**

1 = definitely disagree    4 = tend to agree
2 = tend to disagree    5 = definitely agree
3 = not sure

27. It is my personal responsibility to share the gospel message with non-Christians in my life. 1 2 3 4 5
28. Once a person is saved, he cannot lose his salvation. 1 2 3 4 5
29. I often accept other Christians' constructive criticism and correction. 1 2 3 4 5
30. I believe that the Holy Spirit is active in my life. 1 2 3 4 5
31. If a person sincerely seeks God, she can obtain eternal life through religions other than Christianity. 1 2 3 4 5
32. I know how to explain the gospel clearly to another person without relying on an evangelistic tract. 1 2 3 4 5
33. A Christian should consider himself accountable to other Christians. 1 2 3 4 5
34. A Christian should regularly find ways to tell others about Jesus. 1 2 3 4 5
35. Salvation is available only through receiving Jesus Christ. 1 2 3 4 5
36. The way I live my Christian life is not others' business. 1 2 3 4 5
37. The Holy Spirit comes into a person the moment she accepts Jesus as Savior. 1 2 3 4 5
38. A literal place called hell exists. 1 2 3 4 5
39. I believe that I have a personal responsibility to help the poor and hungry. 1 2 3 4 5
40. The complete indwelling of the Holy Spirit occurs through an experience that is usually separate and distinct from the conversion experience. 1 2 3 4 5

**How many hours during the past month have you done each of the following through church, other organizations, or on your own? Do not count time spent in a paid job. Choose from these responses:**

                        3 = 3–5 hours
1 = 0 hours          4 = 6–9 hours
2 = 1–2 hours     5 = 10 hours or more

41. Donated time helping persons who are poor, hungry, sick, or unable to care for themselves (don't count family members) 1 2 3 4 5
42. Visited those who have visited my church 1 2 3 4 5
43. Helped friends or neighbors with problems 1 2 3 4 5
44. Been involved in a missions-related ministry or cause (for example, teaching about missions, raising money for missions, missions volunteer work) 1 2 3 4 5
45. Visited persons in the hospital 1 2 3 4 5
46. Given volunteer time at my church to teach, lead, serve on a committee, or help with a program or event 1 2 3 4 5
47. Visited in the homes of Christian friends 1 2 3 4 5
48. Visited the elderly or the homebound 1 2 3 4 5

**How true is each of the following statements for you? Choose from these responses:**

1 = absolutely false    4 = mostly true
2 = somewhat false    5 = absolutely true
3 = not sure

49. I am open and responsive to Bible teachers in my church. 1 2 3 4 5
50. I readily receive and forgive those who offend me. 1 2 3 4 5
51. I see myself as loved and valued by God. 1 2 3 4 5
52. I express genuine praise and gratitude to God even in the midst of difficult circumstances. 1 2 3 4 5
53. I avoid close relationships with others who hinder the expression of my Christian values and principles. 1 2 3 4 5
54. I am consciously aware that God placed me on earth to contribute to the fulfillment of His plans and purposes. 1 2 3 4 5
55. I recognize that everything I have belongs to God. 1 2 3 4 5
56. My life is filled with stress and anxiety. 1 2 3 4 5
57. I believe that God will always provide my basic needs in life. 1 2 3 4 5
58. I am somewhat hesitant to let others know that I am a Christian. 1 2 3 4 5
59. I avoid situations in which I might be tempted by sexual immorality. 1 2 3 4 5
60. I am presently struggling with an unforgiving atti-

tude toward another person. **1 2 3 4 5**

61. I feel very inferior to others in my church.
**1 2 3 4 5**

62. I seek God first in expressing my values and setting my priorities. **1 2 3 4 5**

63. I am able to remain confident of God's love and provision even during very difficult circumstances.
**1 2 3 4 5**

64. I forgive those who offend me even if they do not apologize. **1 2 3 4 5**

65. Being a Christian is a private matter and does not need to be discussed with others. **1 2 3 4 5**

**Last year what percentage of your income did you contribute to each of the following? Choose from these responses:**

| | |
|---|---|
| 1 = 0% | 4 = 6–9% |
| 2 = 1–2% | 5 = 10% and above |
| 3 = 3–5% | |

66. To my church **1 2 3 4 5**

67. To other religious groups or religious organizations **1 2 3 4 5**

68. To charities or social-service organizations
**1 2 3 4 5**

69. To international missions (through my church and denomination) **1 2 3 4 5**

**For the following question choose from these responses:**

| | |
|---|---|
| 1 = none | 4 = the majority |
| 2 = a few | 5 = all |
| 3 = several | |

70. How many of your closest friends do you consider to be unbelievers? **1 2 3 4 5**

**How often have you done each of the following during the past year? Choose from these responses:**

| | |
|---|---|
| 1 = never | 4 = 6–9 times |
| 2 = once | 5 = 10 times or more |
| 3 = 2–5 times | |

71. Clearly felt God's presence in my life **1 2 3 4 5**

72. Shared with someone how to become a Christian
**1 2 3 4 5**

73. Invited an unchurched person to attend church, Bible study, or another evangelistic event
**1 2 3 4 5**

74. Experienced the Holy Spirit's providing understanding, guidance, or conviction of sin
**1 2 3 4 5**

75. Met with a new Christian to help him grow spiritually **1 2 3 4 5**

76. Told others about God's work in my life
**1 2 3 4 5**

77. Helped someone pray to receive Christ
**1 2 3 4 5**

78. Gave a gospel tract or similar literature to an unbeliever **1 2 3 4 5**

**Indicate how much you agree or disagree with each of the following. Choose from these responses:**

| | |
|---|---|
| 1 = strongly disagree | 4 = agree |
| 2 = disagree | 5 = strongly agree |
| 3 = not sure | |

79. It is very important for every Christian to serve others. **1 2 3 4 5**

80. One day God will hold me accountable for how I used my time, money, and talents. **1 2 3 4 5**

81. All Christians are to follow Bible teachings.
**1 2 3 4 5**

82. The Bible is the authoritative source of wisdom for daily living. **1 2 3 4 5**

83. A Christian must learn to deny herself to serve Christ effectively. **1 2 3 4 5**

84. I have a hard time accepting myself. **1 2 3 4 5**

85. I have identified my primary spiritual gift.
**1 2 3 4 5**

86. Following death, an unbeliever goes to a place called hell. **1 2 3 4 5**

87. Jesus' teachings are binding for the modern Christian. **1 2 3 4 5**

88. Giving time to a specific ministry in the church is necessary for a Christian's spiritual welfare.
**1 2 3 4 5**

89. Regardless of my circumstances, I believe God always keeps His promises. **1 2 3 4 5**

90. Without the death of Jesus, salvation would not be possible. **1 2 3 4 5**

91. The Bible is a completely reliable revelation from God. **1 2 3 4 5**

**Indicate how well-trained and prepared you believe you are in the following areas. Choose**

from these responses:

1 = not trained at all     4 = adequately
2 = somewhat trained       trained
3 = average       5 = well-trained

92. Presenting the plan of salvation  1 2 3 4 5
93. Individually following up or helping a new Christian grow and develop spiritually  1 2 3 4 5
94. Leading someone to pray to receive Christ  1 2 3 4 5
95. Visiting a prospect for my church  1 2 3 4 5
96. Leading a small-group Bible study  1 2 3 4 5
97. Sharing my personal testimony about how I became a Christian  1 2 3 4 5

**How often during the past two or three years have you done each of the following? Choose from these responses:**

1 = never       4 = weekly
2 = a few times     5 = daily
3 = monthly

98. Read the Bible by myself  1 2 3 4 5
99. Consciously put into practice the teachings of the Bible  1 2 3 4 5
100. Prayed by myself  1 2 3 4 5
101. Provided help to needy persons in my town or city  1 2 3 4 5
102. Read and studied about the Christian faith  1 2 3 4 5
103. Participated in Bible studies, religious programs, or groups outside my church  1 2 3 4 5
104. Made the necessary changes when I realized, as a result of exposure to the Bible, that an aspect of my life was not right  1 2 3 4 5
105. Shared an insight, idea, principle, or guideline from the Bible with others  1 2 3 4 5
106. Experienced the care, love, and support of other persons in a church  1 2 3 4 5
107. Directly tried to encourage someone to believe in Jesus Christ  1 2 3 4 5
108. Intentionally spent time building friendships with non-Christians  1 2 3 4 5

**How true is each of these statements for you? Choose from these responses:**

1 = never true       4 = often true
2 = rarely true       5 = almost always true
3 = sometimes true

109. I feel God's presence in my relationships with other persons.  1 2 3 4 5
110. I treat persons of the other gender in a pure and holy manner.  1 2 3 4 5
111. When convicted of sin in my life, I readily confess it to God as sin.  1 2 3 4 5
112. Through prayer I seek to discern God's will for my life.  1 2 3 4 5
113. I readily forgive others because of my understanding that God has forgiven me.  1 2 3 4 5
114. I help others with their religious questions and struggles.  1 2 3 4 5
115. I have learned through my faith and the Scriptures how to sacrifice for the good of others.  1 2 3 4 5
116. I share my faults and weaknesses with others whom I consider to be close to me.  1 2 3 4 5
117. I am generally the same person in private that I am in public.  1 2 3 4 5
118. When God makes me aware of His specific will for me in an area of my life, I follow His leading.  1 2 3 4 5
119. I regularly find myself choosing God's way over my way in specific instances.  1 2 3 4 5
120. I am honest in my dealings with others.  1 2 3 4 5
121. I regularly pray for my church's ministry.  1 2 3 4 5

**How often do you attend the following activities? Choose from these responses:**

1 = never       4 = weekly
2 = a few times     5 = more than once a week
3 = monthly

122. Worship services at my church  1 2 3 4 5
123. Sunday School class  1 2 3 4 5
124. Bible studies other than Sunday School  1 2 3 4 5
125. Prayer groups or prayer meetings  1 2 3 4 5

**Indicate how much you agree or disagree with each of the following statements. Choose from these responses:**     3 = not sure

1 = definitely disagree     4 = tend to agree
2 = tend to disagree     5 = definitely agree

126. God fulfills His plan primarily through believers within a local-church context.  1 2 3 4 5

127. Christ designated local churches as His means and environment for nurturing believers in the faith. **1 2 3 4 5**

128. A new believer should experience believer's baptism by immersion prior to acceptance by a local church as a member. **1 2 3 4 5**

129. Baptism and the Lord's Supper are local church ordinances and should not be practiced outside the gathered church. **1 2 3 4 5**

130. Each person born into the world inherited a sinful nature as a result of Adam's fall and is thereby separated from God and is in need of a Savior. **1 2 3 4 5**

131. Each local church is autonomous, with Jesus Christ as the Head, and should work together with other churches to spread the gospel to all people. **1 2 3 4 5**

132. There is only one true and personal God, who reveals Himself to humanity as God the Father, God the Son, and God the Holy Spirit. **1 2 3 4 5**

133. Christ will return a second time to receive His believers, living and dead, unto Himself and to bring the world to an appropriate end. **1 2 3 4 5**

134. Jesus Christ is God's Son, who died on the cross for the sins of the world and was resurrected from the dead. **1 2 3 4 5**

135. Jesus Christ, during His incarnate life on earth, was fully God and fully man. **1 2 3 4 5**

136. How religious or spiritual would you say your 3 or 4 best friends are? **1 2 3**
    1 = not very religious
    2 = somewhat religious
    3 = very religious

137. How many of your closest friends are professing Christians? **1 2 3 4 5**
    1 = none          4 = the majority
    2 = a few         5 = all
    3 = several

138. Are you male or female? **Male     Female**

139. Indicate your age group: **1 2 3 4 5**
    1 = 18–22          4 = 41–50
    2 = 23–30          5 = 51–60
    3 = 31–40          6 = 61 and over

140. I have been an active member of a local church. **1 2 3 4 5**

1 = never          4 = a large part of my life
2 = a short time   5 = most of my life
    in my life
3 = about half of
    my life

141. How long have you been a Christian? **1 2 3 4 5 6**
    1 = less than 1 year   4 = 6–10 years
    2 = 1–3 years          5 = 11–20 years
    3 = 4–5 years          6 = More than 20 years

142. Identifying as a member of a local church wherever I live is—**1 2 3 4 5**
    1 = unnecessary    4 = of great value
    2 = of little value  5 = imperative
    3 = of some value

143. Have you ever been involved in discipleship training (an organized, weekly discipleship group)?     **Yes          No**
    If so, which discipleship-training program were you involved in?

144. *MasterLife*                          **Yes          No**
145. Navigators                          **Yes          No**
146. *Survival Kit*                       **Yes          No**
147. Evangelism Explosion               **Yes          No**
148. *Continuing Witness Training*   **Yes          No**
    If other, please provide the name:

    _____

149. How many weeks were you involved in this discipleship training? **1 2 3 4 5**
    1 = 0–5 weeks       4 = 16–25 weeks
    2 = 6–10 weeks      5 = More than 25 weeks
    3 = 11–15 weeks

150. When were you involved in this training?
    From _____ to _____

151. Was this discipleship training sponsored by your local church? **Yes     No**
    If not, what group or organization sponsored the training?_____

152. Have you ever been discipled one-to-one by another Christian?     **Yes          No**

[1]James Slack and Brad Waggoner, "The Discipleship Inventory" (Richmond: The International Mission Board of the Southern Baptist Convention). Used by permission.

# CHRISTIAN GROWTH STUDY PLAN

*Preparing Christians to Serve*

In the **Christian Growth Study Plan (formerly the Church Study Course)** *MasterLife 1: The Disciple's Cross* is a resource for course credit in the subject area Personal Life in the Christian Growth category of diploma plans. To receive credit, read the book; complete the learning activities; attend group sessions; show your work to your pastor, a staff member, or a church leader; and complete the following information. This page may be duplicated. Send the completed page to:

**Christian Growth Study Plan**
**127 Ninth Avenue, North, MSN 117**
**Nashville, TN 37234-0117**
**FAX: (615) 251-5067**

For information about the Christian Growth Study Plan, refer to the current *Christian Growth Study Plan Catalog.* Your church office may have a copy. If not, request a free copy from the Christian Growth Study Plan office, (615) 251-2525.

## MasterLife 1: The Disciple's Cross
### COURSE NUMBER: CG-0168

**PARTICIPANT INFORMATION**

| Social Security Number | Personal CGSP Number* | Date of Birth |
|---|---|---|

| Name (First, MI, Last) | | Home Phone |
|---|---|---|
| ☐Mr.　☐Miss | | |
| ☐Mrs.　☐ | | |

| Address (Street, Route, or P.O. Box) | City, State | ZIP |
|---|---|---|

**CHURCH INFORMATION**

| Church Name |
|---|

| Address (Street, Route, or P.O. Box) | City, State | ZIP |
|---|---|---|

**CHANGE REQUEST ONLY**

| ☐Former Name |
|---|

| ☐Former Address | City, State | ZIP |
|---|---|---|

| ☐Former Church | City, State | ZIP |
|---|---|---|

| Signature of Pastor, Conference Leader, or Other Church Leader | Date |
|---|---|

*New participants are requested but not required to give SS# and date of birth. Existing participants, please give CGSP# when using SS# for the first time. Thereafter, only one ID# is required. *Mail to:* Christian Growth Study Plan, 127 Ninth Ave., North, MSN 117, Nashville, TN 37234-0117. Fax: (615) 251-5067.